A Walk Along Penn Yan's Main Street

Susan U. Lange

Yates Heritage Tours Project, LLC

Dundee, NY

Other publications by the Yates Heritage Tours Project, LLC

The Unquiet World: The Public Universal Friend & America's First Frontier by Frances Dumas, Yates County Historian, 2010, ISBN: 978-0-9828058-0-0

The Universal Friend and America's First Frontier Settlement 1780 - 1820 — A Self-Guided Audio Driving Tour of Historic Sites in Yates County, New York. Edited by County Historian, Frances Dumas, 2010, ISBN: 978-0-9828058-1-7

Architecture in a Small Town — A tour of Architectural Styles in the Village of Penn Yan, New York Compiled by Sue Lange, 2011, ISBN: 978-0-9828058-2-4

Historic Penn Yan, A Coloring and Activity Book by Susan U. Lange, 2011

Cover Images:

The top postcard is the west side of Main Street in 1868. The view is from the corner of Elm and Main Streets, looking south, with the Armstrong & Gage Hardware in the foreground.

The second postcard shows Penn Yan's Main Street in the 1920s. This picture was taken from the north end of the commercial district near Maiden Lane and the current Jacob Street, looking south. Main Street is brick paved with vehicles all parked on the diagonal. Penn Yan was a thriving community.

Abraham Wagener, considered to be the founder of Penn Yan, is shown in his later years.

All these images are courtesy of the Yates County Genealogical & Historical Society.

Cover design by Steve Knapp, www.Keukaview.com

First printing, June 2012
Second printing, July 2012
Third printing, October 2012
Fourth printing, December 2012

ISBN #978-0-9828058-3-1

Library of Congress Control Number: 2012940373

Yates Heritage Tours Project, LLC
971 East Lake Road
Dundee, New York 14837
email: YatesHeritageTours@gmail.com
Website: YatesHeritageTours.com

Table of Contents

Acknowledgements

Yates Heritage Tours Project focuses on capturing the history of the Finger Lakes region, and then putting it into a format such that residents and visitors alike can appreciate and learn from. Like many small villages, Penn Yan has an interesting history. We are fortunate that so many of the early buildings remain today. In addition, the community has had many citizens who valued history and who both retained it and passed it on to future generations. The Yates County Genealogical & Historical Society has a wealth of information. Their staff, in particular Lisa Harper and Chuck Mitchell, have been of great assistance to me while I used their facilities for research in gathering the material and many of the old photographs that you will find in this book. In addition, I would like to thank friends and neighbors Bob Scharf and Tom Packard who have shared items from their private collections of the history of the area which helped enhance the tour.

I also want to extend my great appreciation to my support team: my husband Jerry Lange, took most of the new photographs found in this book, digitally enhanced all the images and put the material into the software that made this a usable book; Sid Mann also contributed photographs, created the map that you will use for the tour, and proofed the copy; Steve Knapp used his design skills to create the cover; and Frances Dumas, Yates County Historian as well as the local public historian of Penn Yan and Milo, graciously checked all the facts. Without their help this book would never have come to be.

History is in the eye of the beholder. I have done my best to make sure that this document is accurate. I hope that you will enjoy it as much as I have enjoyed creating it.

Sue Lange

June 2012

An Introduction To
A Walk Along Penn Yan's Main Street

The Village of Penn Yan is located in the Finger Lakes region of New York State, in Yates County, nestled along the edge of the east leg of Keuka Lake. Indians hunted here years before the first white settlers arrived. In the late 1700s people came from Pennsylvania and New England in hopes of finding the beautiful wilderness promised by those who had visited the area during the Revolutionary War's Sullivan – Clinton Campaign in 1779. These brave settlers were told that there was plenty of water provided by lakes and streams, woods filled with wildlife and timber, and fertile soil. Imagine traveling over the hills, along raging rivers and through dense forests carrying all your belongings to start a new life. Start a new life they did. They cleared land so that they could plant crops and provide food for themselves. They built log cabins. They built mills, taverns, schools and churches. Before long they had created a village which was to become the seat of the county of Yates. The story of the people who came before us and created all that we now enjoy is an interesting one. We will be telling it as we walk along the Main Street of Penn Yan.

We welcome you to a walking tour of Penn Yan's Historic Main Street. Main Street is part of the village's historic preservation district. The district also includes: Chapel Street from Main Street to Liberty Street, Clinton Street from Main Street to just beyond Collins Avenue, Court Street west to Liberty Street, a portion of Elm Street, Wagener Street and Water Street. It is because of this historic district that Penn Yan still has so many wonderful buildings.

This tour book includes: a brief history of Penn Yan's early years covering the village's beginning up into the 1930s; a map of Main Street indicating the blocks where various buildings appear; a time line to enable you to easily determine what was happening during the year each building was constructed, and images of each building as it once appeared, when possible, and as it is today, along with details about the building. Through these buildings you will learn the story of the Village of Penn Yan.

If you have children under the age of 12 you will want to review the Children's Scavenger Hunt which appears at the back of the book. Answers to Scavenger Hunt questions can be found in Penn Yan's Historic Commercial District. Once your child has answered all the questions, remove the form and return it to Longs' Cards & Books at 115 Main Street, Penn Yan to pick up your prize of one copy of the *Historic Penn Yan, A Coloring and Activity Book*. There is a limit of one prize per tour.

Our tour begins and ends near the Penn Yan Post Office. Public parking is conveniently available in a lot off Maiden Lane or one off Jacob Street, behind Longs' Cards & Books. For the tour of the Commercial District you will walk from in front of the Struble's Arcade, 144-150 Main Street, south on the west side of Main Street. You will then cross the street just before the bridge at Birkett Mills and return on the east side of the street to the Post Office. For the tour of the Residential District you will start at 158 Main Street, Fox Inn Bed & Breakfast and walk north on the west side of Main Street. When you arrive at North Avenue you will cross the street again and return to the Post Office by walking south on the east side of the street. Main Street is less than a mile long from the Outlet to North Avenue.

If you have an interest in architecture we suggest that you purchase a copy of *Architecture in a Small Town*, our companion book about architectural styles during the period of 1790 through today. Each style has a listing of characteristics. There are illustrations of structures which exemplify each style, a glossary of architectural terms and a map which will help you locate each example. This book is available in Penn Yan through Longs' Cards & Books, the Yates County Genealogical & Historical Society, the Pinwheel Market & Cafe or directly through Yates Heritage Tours Project, YatesHeritageTours@gmail.com.

Learning about Penn Yan's history and the people who created it can be fascinating. In *A Walk Along Penn Yan's Main Street* we only address some of the highlights. If you want to learn more of the story be sure to pick up a copy of Frances Dumas's book, *Penn Yan & How It Got That Way*. Fran's book tells the complete story from the geological beginning of this area to the current day. With it you will discover much more about Penn Yan's story, how it came to be and what this little village has contributed to our region and the nation.

Before you begin your walk along Penn Yan's Main Street we suggest that you familiarize yourself with the tour book and read the section on Penn Yan's early history.

The Early History of the Village of Penn Yan

In this section we will review some highlights of the village's history from its early settlement in the late 1700s till the late 1930s. Much has happened here in the more than 200 years since the first settlers arrived. Penn Yan, like many villages settled during the late 1700s, was located near water, by people who were moving west in search of a better place to live.

The first people to make this their home came thousands of years ago. They are thought to have migrated from Asia, crossing the Bering Straits and arriving here about 4,000 BC. These nomadic hunter-gatherers followed herds of animals which they killed for food, tools and clothing. They found this region to be rich with wildlife, and an abundance of fresh water, fertile soil and timber. The Seneca Nation, a part of the Six Nation Iroquois Confederacy called the Haudenosaunee or the "People of the Longhouse," were the last of the native people to settle here. They built a village on the western shore of Seneca Lake south of Geneva at Kashong. It had a beautiful apple orchard and log homes. One of the officers in the Sullivan Campaign in 1779 reported in his journal that some of the homes even had glass windows.

In 1763 the British drew a line which prohibited colonials from settling west of the Appalachian

Boundary between Mississippi River and 49th parallel uncertain due to misconception that source of Mississippi River lay further north

1775

The Proclamation Line of 1763. This map shows North America in 1775. The Proclamation line is clearly indicated. Note the Indian Reserve to the west of it. The thirteen British colonies are all on the east side of the line. In this way they remained dependent on British trade. Unfortunately the land on the east, especially in New England, was rapidly filling up. The Indian land to the west was perfect for settlement. (YCH)

3

Mountains. It was called the Proclamation Line. The intent was to keep the colonials along the east coast making it more likely that they would continue to trade with the British. The Proclamation Line would also help prevent conflicts between the Indians and colonials who might want the same land. This line was one of many issues that led to the Revolutionary War.

In 1779 during the Revolutionary War's Sullivan – Clinton Campaign, the small Indian village at Kashong, along with many other Seneca towns, was destroyed by the Colonial army led by Major General John Sullivan and General James Clinton. General George Washington ordered the destruction of the Senecas as retaliation for the 1778 Indian and Tory raids on the colonial settlements of Cherry Valley, New York located near the Mohawk River, and Wyoming, Pennsylvania on the Susquehanna River near Wilkes Barre. The first battle of the Sullivan Campaign occurred at Newtown, New York (south of Elmira). From there the army of 5100 men moved north up the Catharine Valley, south of Seneca Lake to Montour Falls, along the east side of Seneca Lake, then west of Geneva, with a detour south by 400 soldiers to Kashong, and then on to Canandaigua, Honeoye and Hemlock Lakes. Finally, they went south of Conesus Lake and then on to the Genesee River, destroying the Indians' homes, orchards and crops, and releasing any livestock that the Indians left behind as they fled. Another group went east to Albany traveling through Auburn and Skaneateles. The Indians in this region of New York fled first to Fort Niagara and the protection of their British allies. Here they spent a horrible winter. Later some of the Indians migrated west or into Canada.

The Sullivan Campaign made the region safer for settlement. Men who had been a part of the campaign returned home and told of how special this region was.

In 1787 a group of three men, followers of **Jemima Wilkinson**, the Public Universal Friend, visited the region, then called the Genesee Country, looking for a place to settle. Jemima was the first American born woman to found a religious movement. The early European settlers of this new nation had used up much of the good farmland along the east coast and were looking for more. Just as Sullivan and Clinton's men had before them, they found the region to be a beautiful wilderness. Some say that they found two French-Canadian traders and their Cayuga wives at Kashong and at Indian Pines a man who may have been of French or Spanish descent who repaired firearms for the Indians. Still another man named Jacob

Fredenburgh, a survivor of Shay's rebellion, lived in a log cabin on a hill south of what would become Penn Yan where Brown and South Avenue are today. He had made friends with the Indians who allowed him to hunt and fish. He told the scouts that no other white people lived in the area. The scouts returned to Pennsylvania where they told the Universal Friends about what they had found.

In December 1786 the Treaty of Hartford had been signed. This treaty settled the dispute between New York and Massachusetts over who owned this land. It gave Massachusetts the pre-emptive right (the right to buy out the Senecas) and gave New York sovereignty (the right to collect taxes).

During the summer of 1788, shortly after the United States Constitution was ratified, the Haudenosaunee signed a treaty to transfer the preemptive rights of 6,000,000 acres of land to Massachusetts who sold it to the Phelps and Gorham Company. Phelps and Gorham owed Massachusetts one million dollars. The region was officially open for white settlement. The eastern boundary was determined by a survey which created the Pre-Emption Line. It was drawn from the eighty second mile stone on the northeast border of Pennsylvania and New York, up along the western side of Seneca Lake to Sodus on Lake Ontario. Somehow as it was drawn the line moved about 2 miles west of where it should have been. Years later another survey corrected the line and the gap between the two lines was called the Gore. This change caused the ownership of land within the Gore to be in question.

In August, that same summer, a group of twenty-five of Jemima Wilkinson's followers, the Universal Friends, arrived from Connecticut on the western shores of Seneca Lake just south of Kashong Creek in what is now the town of Torrey. They had traveled up the Hudson River and then west to Seneca Lake. Later more Universal Friends followed the Sullivan-Clinton campaign route from Pennsylvania. Here they created the first organized white settlement in the Genesee Country. By 1790 the Universal Friends had a settlement of almost 300 people. They settled at City Hill, Milo Center and along the Keuka Lake Outlet. The story of Jemima Wilkinson, also known as the Public Universal Friend, and this first settlement is told in a fascinating book written by Yates County Historian, Frances Dumas titled *The Unquiet World, The Public Universal Friend and America's First Frontier*, and in a self-guided audio driving tour titled *The Universal Friend and America's First Frontier Settlement 1780 -1820*. Look for both at Longs' Cards & Books and The Pinwheel

Market & Cafe on Main Street, the Yates County Genealogical & Historical Society on Chapel Street in Penn Yan or through Yates Heritage Tours Project. In addition, the Yates County Genealogical & Historical Society, on Chapel Street in Penn Yan, has a wonderful exhibit on Jemima Wilkinson and the Universal Friends. Stop by the Underwood House Museum Tuesday through Friday to visit.

The Phelps-Gorham Purchase included the land that would become Penn Yan. Phelps had their purchase surveyed and divided it into tracts with ranges running north and south. Divided into townships six miles square, they were numbered northward toward lake Ontario one to fourteen. The ranges were numbered westerly from one to seven. They ceded towns 6, 7 and 8 in the first range, along with 9 in the second range, to the Lessees at the meeting in Buffalo with the Indians. 6, 7 and 8 were Barrington, Milo and Benton. Phelps and Gorham began to sell the lots in the remainder of the land they had acquired. Many people who purchased land along the west side of Seneca Lake later discovered that the survey was wrong and the land they thought they owned was on the wrong side of the Pre-Emption Line. In 1790, Phelps was unable to make his payment to Massachusetts. So, in 1791 Massachusetts sold the land to Robert Morris. He sold it to the Pulteney Estate in 1792. A new survey, which corrected the Pre-Emption Line, was then conducted. For a detailed discussion of these land transactions refer to Frances Dumas' book *The Unquiet World*.

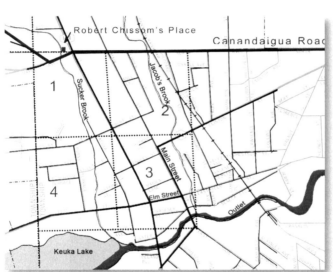

Penn Yan. This map indicates the four quarters that divided lot 37 between Robert Chissom and James Scofield. Numbers 1 and 3 were given to Robert Chissom while 2 and 4 were given to James Scofield. (SM)

On November 11th, 1794 the Canandaigua Treaty was signed between some of the nations of the Haudenosaunee and the U.S. government. Red Jacket and Corn Planter were two of the Indians present. Timothy Pickering was the agent for President George Washington. This treaty established land rights for the Indians along with the boundaries of the Phelps and Gorham Purchase. That treaty is still in effect today. Per the treaty the United States government pays the Indians $4,500 each year for an annual distribution of cloth. A celebration commemorates the treaty each year at Canandaigua on November 11th, when the annual payment is made.

Charles Williamson, the Pulteney Estate's agent, was anxious to fill up the region as quickly as possible. He thought settlers would flock here from the south around the Chesapeake and up along the Susquehanna River. The migration to this region instead came primarily from northeast Pennsylvania and New England and was the first western movement after the settlement of the new world by European pioneers. Williamson was right, settlers were anxious to move to the new frontier. Williamson was a good salesman and was instrumental in making many changes to the region. He built roads, taverns and inns to make travel easier. He had a vision of the region which included a major city at Bath. It was there that he put his headquarters and land office. A road was created from Bath through Geneva to Sodus. A portion of that road is still in use and is called the Old Bath Road. It goes south from Penn Yan through Wayne and on towards Hammondsport. The original road went through Milo Center west to Bath Road and existed before the Village of Penn Yan.

Meanwhile in 1791, **George Wheeler**, a wealthy Benton settler, purchased lot 37 of Township 7, in the first range. It consisted of 276 acres which was to become Penn Yan. In January 1792 he divided lot 37 between his two sons-in-law. He gave James Scofield the northeast and southwest quarters. He gave Robert Chissom the northwest and southeast quarters. You can see this division on the map pictured on the previous page. These two early settlers built homes on the western parts of their land. Chissom built on what is now Maple Avenue. His home became Penn Yan's first tavern. He also built a distillery. His daughter Catherine was the first child born in the village. Scofield built a log house near Sucker Brook, north of Elm Street.

The tax roll of 1792 shows that Chissom sold the southern part of his land to Lewis Birdsall. Birdsall hired millwright, Enoch Malin, to build him a dam and sawmill on the Outlet.

David Wagener, a friend of Jemima Wilkinson, had moved to the area from Montgomery County, Pennsylvania in 1791. He became part owner of the Friend's grist mill on the Outlet. Later he purchased the southeast corner of lot 37, including Birdsall's mill lot, and added both a grist mill and a house which was also used as a tavern. In 1796 David acquired two more quarters so that he owned three-quarters of lot 37.

About 1795 David Wagener, who believed the new settlement needed a doctor, gave Pennsylvanian **Dr. John Dorman** some land to encourage him to join the others living here. Dr. Dorman's property was the section located on the east side of the current Main Street between East Elm Street and Seneca Street. Dr. Dorman built an elaborate two story log building. The top floor opened onto the trail that would become Main Street. The lower level opened out on to the bank of Jacob's Brook. The bank of the brook was steep, so it was easy to have both floors open onto land. This building later became a distillery and tavern operated by Dorman's son Aaron Gilbert Dorman. Over a period of time Aaron had three distilleries.

By 1796 the Pulteney Associates agent Charles Williamson's hard work had paid off and the population of the area was large enough for Ontario County to be split. Ontario County had been organized in 1789 with Canandaigua as the county seat. At that time it was geographically a huge county as the population of this region was small. When the southern part was split off into Steuben County the new county's seat was established in Bath, just as Williamson had imagined.

In 1799 the trail that became Main Street was surveyed through the swamp of lower Main Street. It was a while before any buildings of significance were built at the lower end of Main Street. In 1820, if you stood in front of today's Post Office and looked south along Main Street toward the Outlet you would have seen a swampy, muddy area where little grew except scrub pines, some bushes and an occasional pine tree. Imagine a dirt road just wide enough for a wagon. The mills were at the south end of the road. Some taverns, stores and homes were located at the north end.

Because it was so wet and swampy, the area starting at the foot of Keuka Lake and along the Outlet was not attractive for settlement. In fact some considered it to be an unhealthy environment. In August 1799 David Wagener died unexpectedly. He was only 47. His was the first burial in a plot of land he had donated to the community for a cemetery. Penn Yan would later purchase more land from Abraham Wagener and his son Charles and create what is now known as Lakeview Cemetery. David left his gristmill and his home, along with the care of his wife, to his younger son Melchoir. He left the rest of his land, north of the Outlet, to his oldest son, Abraham.

In 1799 **Abraham Wagener** built the first frame house in Penn Yan near Chapel Street on the east side of Main Street. He moved in on New Year's day 1800. Dr. Dorman also built a frame house early in 1800. His was the second frame house in Penn Yan. It was painted red and was located on Main Street where Community Bank stands today. Abraham constructed a second grist mill on the north side of the Outlet in 1801. It was also that year that he became the village's first postmaster. The post office was in his house. It went by the name of Jerusalem as Penn Yan was yet to be named. Jerusalem was named by Jemima Wilkinson and the Universal Friends when they left the Gore and moved west. Their first settlement was Jerusalem as was their second. Penn Yan was a part of Jerusalem as were Benton, Milo and Torrey until 1802. Penn Yan's population grew and the village was finally named. Abraham held the office of postmaster for 14 years.

The Mansion House. A drawing of the Mansion House after it was moved south closer toward the bank of the Outlet. It is likely that the section toward the back was the original house. The portion to the right was an addition. You can just see attached to the right side number 10–12 Main Street which is the Keuka Restaurant. (YCGHS)

In 1801 Abraham had a road cut from Canandaigua to Newtown (now known as Elmira). It went east to the north end of Seneca Lake then south and was used as a mail route. In 1808 Abraham was appointed to the position of justice of the peace, an office which he held for 26 years.

In 1813, he built another house. Much more elaborate than his first, it was called the Mansion House. It was located on the west side of Main Street north of where the Knapp Hotel stands today. This home was a farm and had an extensive apple orchard. It is said that Abraham's father, David, planted the seedling which became the Wagener apple and was grown there.

In 1823, wanting Penn Yan to become the new Yates County seat, Abraham is said to have given the county the two acre parcel where the county buildings are located today. However, the actual deed

Abraham Wagener in his later years. (YCGHS)

Abraham Wagener's House on Bluff Point. This is the house that Abraham moved to at the end of Bluff Point. It has a wonderful view of Keuka Lake. (YCGHS)

shows a consideration of $5,000. Jerusalem and Dresden also wanted to be the county seat. Some men from Penn Yan actively campaigned to obtain the seat. Penn Yan was centrally located and Abraham helped encourage the selection of Penn Yan with his "donation" of land. Though Abraham was generous in his donations of land for public places, he also sold off a good portion of his land.

In 1832 Abraham bought 1100 acres on Bluff Point. When the village was incorporated in 1833 he became its first mayor. He is said to have named several of the village's streets – Main, Liberty, Court, Chapel, Jacob (East Elm), Elm, Canal (now Seneca) and Pine (now Keuka). In 1836, he sold the rest of his property in the village, this time to a syndicate led by John Sloan of Geneva. Abraham moved, with his second wife, out to his new home, a stone mansion at the end of the Bluff. If you drive to the end of the Bluff along Skyline Drive you can see that mansion as it looks today. The property Abraham sold to John Sloan was a section east of Liberty Street and south of Elm and Jacob Streets (Jacob Street is now East Elm Street). It included the mills and the Mansion House. Sloan created Wagener Street. The Mansion House was moved south to make room for building lots.

Abraham returned to Penn Yan from his home on the Bluff in 1844 and lived in the stone house at the top of Court Street until he died in 1854. He is considered to be the founder of Penn Yan and, as he was a justice of the peace, is often called "Squire" Wagener.

On the **1800** census there were only nine households listed in Penn Yan. By 1810 there were twenty, with two settlements – one at each end of Main Street. At this time Main Street was the road between the taverns at the north end and the mills at the south along the Outlet. The street was not officially named until 1833, though it was called Main Street for years before. Still, Penn Yan was the center of the surrounding countryside. At the north end of the street along with the taverns, there were two stores and a few homes. Head Street was a stage coach route. Stage coaches came through on their way to and from Geneva and Bath. Generally they stopped twice a week at which time they would bring newspapers, if available, and mail. At the other end of the street were two gristmills, two sawmills, a store located in the red clapboard house (the second frame house in the village) built by Dr. Dorman, Gilbert Dorman's tavern, and a few homes, mainly log, located along the bank of Jacob's Brook. Penn Yan had a reputation for being devoted to whisky. It seems to have been distilled in large quantities everywhere.

The population of this area was small in 1812. Still in his book *Military History of Yates County,* Walter Wolcott lists a total of 77 Yates County men who fought in the **War of 1812**. Twenty-eight of those men are buried in the Lakeview cemetery in Penn Yan. Some names which are familiar to our history of Main Street include: Asa Cole, Dr. William Cornwell, Amasa Holden, his son Amasa Holden Jr. and Morris F. Sheppard. Wolcott quoted a speech given by John L. Lewis in 1860 where he stated that the territory which includes Yates county furnished a larger portion of officers and soldiers for the war than any other section of the state. No battles were fought in this area. People learned about the end of the war on January 8, 1815 though the Treaty of Ghent was signed on December 24, 1814.

By **1815** Penn Yan had about 40 houses and 300 residents. The single street was about a mile long. There were three stores, three gristmills, three sawmills, a hotel, two taverns, three tanneries and a saddler, along with shoemakers, carpenters, blacksmiths, joiners, hatters and a potter. There was even a new bridge crossing the Outlet near the dam.

In May 1818 Abraham H. Bennett started Penn Yan's first newspaper, the Penn Yan Herald. At first he mainly copied the news that arrived in newspapers on the stagecoach. The paper's name was changed to the Penn Yan Democrat in 1822. The proprietors were then Bennett and Reed.

Liberty Street School. This school was built about 1893 on Liberty Street for grades 1-8. An addition was made to the rear in the early 1900s. (YCGHS)

Education was important to the new settlers. The first school in the area was built by the Universal Friends in 1796. It was a log meetinghouse, located in Torrey, that was also used as a school. Sarah Richards was the first teacher. The next teacher, in 1797, was Ruth Pritchard. When she married she moved to Penn Yan and continued to teach school in her home. In 1812 a schoolhouse was located on Main Street on the southeast corner of the lot where the Academy was built in 1859. That area is currently behind the middle school and is used as an athletic field. It was at the 1812 schoolhouse that School Master John L. Lewis Sr. first taught school in Penn Yan in 1815. The building was in poor condition in 1820.

Penn Yan Academy. This is an image from the Yates County Atlas of 1876 depicting the Academy which was built by C.V. Bush in 1859 facing Main Street.

Lake Street School. (YCGHS)

In 1829 Yates County Academy & Female Seminary was located in the building which had been the Washington House. It was located on the east side of Main Street opposite the county buildings. The Washington House was a tavern built by Eliah Holcomb, a former

Penn Yan Academy, a photograph of the same 1859 building. (YCGHS)

sea captain. The school had approximately 70 students. There was a boarding house attached to the school which could board about 50 students. By 1834 there were 341 students with 8 teachers. The students paid tuition. Around 1830 a brick school, located on the west side of Liberty Street a little north of the original Academy

Penn Yan Academy. This is a postcard with the image of Penn Yan Academy which was built in 1905. (YCGHS)

lot, replaced the old wooden school where Lewis first taught. It was used until 1843. A frame building was built on Head Street around 1843 and used as a school. Another school was built on Maiden Lane about that time as well. In 1857 the legislature passed an act which incorporated the Penn Yan Union School District. In 1859 Charles V. Bush built the Penn Yan Academy. Bush's school included two large school rooms, 5 recitation rooms, a chapel, a laboratory, a library and a music room. It had 293 students – 126 boys and 167 girls. In 1874 New York State passed its first compulsory school law.

St. Michael's Roman Catholic School opened in 1883. In 1889 there were five Penn Yan schools located at: Head Street, Maiden Lane, Chestnut Street, Lake Street and the Academy on Main Street. Folsom's Business College was located in the Arcade. Keuka College was built in Keuka Park in 1890. More about that later. In 1893 a new Liberty Street School opened. It was located on the Liberty Street side of the Acadamy lot and was used for elementary grades. In 1905, Penn Yan Academy was rebuilt around the original 1859 Academy and made large enough to hold over 500 students. In 1928 there was a debate on whether or not to purchase property for a new school. The anticipated expense was $317,000. The debate went on and finally it was agreed to spend $399,000 on a new junior high school with a capacity for 850 students, alterations to the Academy (high school) for $2,500, alterations to the Liberty Street school for $3,000, a new boiler room, coal storage and a stack for $10,000, boiler room equipment and distribution for $20,000 and finally sites and a playground for $30,500. This all added up to $465,000. A lot of money in 1928. As the years have gone by Penn Yan's schools have continued to change to keep up with the times.

Returning to **1820**, we find that at that time the Outlet had seven gristmills, fourteen sawmills, an oil mill, four carding machines, two trip-hammers and several distilleries which processed local wheat, timber, flaxseed, wool and corn. The water power on the Outlet helped make Penn Yan prosperous and was instrumental in the area being selected for settlement to begin with. Still, in 1820 the village remained concentrated at the two ends of Main Street. However side streets were beginning to be developed.

A new County. As explained earlier, Penn Yan was originally part of Ontario County. In late 1822, a petition asking for this area to become a separate county, to be named Yates, was presented to the State legislature. Joseph Yates, had just been elected governor of New York. The request was granted in 1823. The new county was made up of the townships of Benton, Italy, Jerusalem, Middlesex and Milo. Yates County had a population of 11,000. In 1826, Barrington, Starkey and Harpendings Corners were annexed from Steuben County. Harpendings Corners was located on the edge of Barrington and later became the Village of Dundee. When Yates County was formed in 1823 Penn Yan became the county seat. As previously mentioned, Abraham Wagener wanted Penn Yan to become the county seat so he "donated", or sold, two acres of swampy land half way down Main Street for the county buildings. It is said that the public park where the bandstand now resides was so wet that bull frogs made their home there. It was drained so that the land could be used for public functions.

Some businesses were located on the west side of Main Street just north of Elm Street. This section, numbers 102 to 124, was later called "Brimstone Row." Yet in 1823 most Penn Yan businesses were still located at Head Street. It wasn't until 1833 that the business blocks were more or less continuous in the Main and Elm business area. The businesses located in Brimstone Row were entirely destroyed by a fire in 1836.

Religion. Like education, religion was also important to the early settlers. The first church to be built in Penn Yan was the ***First Presbyterian Church.*** It was organized February 18, 1823. The building was completed in 1824. It was located at 305 Main Street on land given to the church by Dr. William Cornwell and Henry Plympton. In 1841 there was a disagreement among the parishioners about the use of wine at communion and whether slavery was right or wrong. One hundred members withdrew and founded the Union Free Congregational Church of Penn Yan. Their building was constructed at the corner of Main Street and Chapel Street. In 1855 they disbanded and the property was bought by the Methodist Church. A new Presbyterian Church was built at Main Street and Clinton in 1879. It could seat 1000 people. In April 1957 the church was destroyed by fire. The building that you see now was built in 1959.

The **Methodist Church.** Services were occasionally conducted by Reverend Abner Chase at the schoolhouse in the 1820s. In 1824 Abraham Wagener donated land on Chapel Street for a church. In 1826 the Methodist Chapel was built. Revival meetings in the 1830s and 40s brought in some 50 converts. But others withdrew in the 1840s over the abolition of slavery. In 1857 the church had outgrown the chapel so they purchased the Congregational Church located at the corner of Main and Chapel. They sold the first church on Chapel Street in 1872. Then in 1896 they decided to build a new church. While it was being built they met at the County Court House. The new church, costing about $35,000 was dedicated on January 12, 1898. In 1921 the Methodists added steam heat, electric lights and modernized the dining room. In 1928 they expanded the basement. In 1958 they were able to purchase more property to provide more classroom space, offices and meeting rooms, as well as additional parking. A new educational wing was built in 1971.

The first **Baptist** preaching in Penn Yan was in 1811 by Elder Simon Sutherland and Samuel Carpenter. The decision to form a Baptist Society did not occur until 1828. The church was organized in 1830. At first they met in the schoolhouse on Liberty Street. They also met in the Masonic Hall and then in the Court House, till it burned. Next they met in Abraham Bennett's printing office. Their first building was built in 1835. A new church was built in 1871 on the site of the old one. In the late 1890s there were problems with the magnificent 120 foot steeple and it was removed. Six years later the steeple we see today was added to the church.

Penn Yan's **Roman Catholic Church** came to be as a result of Thomas Hendrick. He came to America from Ireland in 1847. On arriving in Penn Yan he went to work at the Anson Wyman market. He later opened a market of his own. Disappointed that there was no Catholic Church in Penn Yan he raised funds to build one. Abraham Wagener donated the land on Keuka Street aproximatly where St. Michael's School is today. In 1850 St. Michael's Roman Catholic Church was dedicated. The church you see on Liberty Street today was built in 1902. It can hold 1000 people.

Returning to the 1820s. In December 1824 the village's second newspaper, called the Yates Republican, was established by Edward J. Powle. It had several different owners over the years. In 1856 its name was changed to the Yates County Chronicle, owned by Stafford Cleveland. In 1926 the Yates County Chronicle merged with the Penn Yan Express to become the Chronicle Express, the paper we are familiar with today.

You will see that **Samuel F. Curtiss** was involved in several of the structures in Penn Yan. He arrived in Penn Yan in 1824 with a wagon load of stock goods. He rented a room from Sheldon & Babcock and space for a store at the corner of Main and Head Streets. An enterprising young man, he immediately began selling chairs. As demand increased he built his first factory on the west side of Main Street. In 1836 he built a four story shop with a sales room at the south corner of Main and Clinton Streets. He made furniture and coffins. In 1858 his son Perley joined the business and they expanded even more. Six years later they built a separate factory. A fire in 1867 destroyed all their buildings. They quickly purchased a three story brick building on Main Street and added a story. In 1869 they purchased the shoe store that Perley ran. Samuel retired in 1870. He was known for his support of the both the abolition and temperance movements. Perley continued these businesses till 1882 when he became a partner with W. H. Fox in the Fox's paper mill. He was also part of the group who in 1884 created the railroad along the Outlet and Canal.

Penn Yan continued to grow. In **1825** there were three general merchants, three insurance agents, an apothecary, three blacksmiths, three lawyers, three physicians (one of whom was also a lawyer), a printer, a harness maker, a carriage maker, three tailors, a hatter, a barber, two innkeepers, two plow dealers, a real estate agent, a clothing works, a cabinetmaker, a furniture maker, a dancing master and a fulling mill. There were 70 houses in the village.

A **religious revival** swept the village in 1826. From that came a local temperance movement. On the 4th of July in 1828 Henry Bradley gave a spirited talk at the Presbyterian meeting house and the County's first temperance society was formed.

Banks. The first bank to come to Penn Yan was the Yates County Bank. It was established in 1831 by William M. Oliver. It was first located in his small law office next to his house. Other prominent men who were part of the bank included: Dr. Andrew

Oliver, Abraham Bennett, George Young, Eben Smith, Samuel S. Ellsworth, Asa Cole and several others. The bank moved to where Lown's is located today around 1833. It was in existence until the crash of 1857. Farmers Bank of Penn Yan was chartered in 1839 and went out of business in 1843. The next bank to be chartered was the Bank of Bainbridge. Chartered by the state in 1847, it became a local bank in 1849. J. T. Rapalee opened a bank with his name in 1860 taking over the building used by the Yates County Bank. In 1869 Mason L. Baldwin started a private banking house. Then in 1881 it was organized as Baldwin's Bank and became one of western New York's leading banks. It was located at 127 Main Street in the Maxwell Building. The First National Bank of Penn Yan was chartered in 1873. It closed in 1899. Yates County National Bank was incorporated the end of 1878. Its board of directors included some familiar Penn Yan names: Dr. Andrew Oliver, Charles C. Sheppard, Nelson Thompson, John Lewis, Morris F. Sheppard, George R. Cornwell and others. The Citizens Bank was organized in 1899. In 1900 it took over, remodeled and enlarged the location formerly used by the First National Bank on the west side of Main Street.

Map of the Canal and the Outlet. This map is from the 1876 Yates County Atlas. You can see how the Canal and the Outlet were separate. The Outlet appears on the top of the map, on the south side. The Canal is on the village or north side of the map.

Canal building fever took hold after the Erie Canal was completed in 1825. A petition was presented to the State legislature by the residents of Yates County requesting that a canal be cut between Seneca Lake and Keuka Lake. Everyone realized what a boon that would be — population growth as well as the opportunity for goods to reach larger markets. The Crooked Lake Canal connecting Penn Yan to Seneca Lake was surveyed in 1828 and completed in 1833. It had 27 lift locks and a guard lock in Penn Yan that allowed boats to

17

Penn Yan harbor about 1905. Sucker Brook is coming in from the right and you can see warehouses on the left. The maps on pages 6 and 17 show the harbor leading to the canal and the Outlet. The Fruit House, the sloped roof building in the distance on the left side of the Outlet, today is Carey's Lumber, the sole remaining building.(YCGHS)

negotiate a 270 foot altitude change in six short miles. The Canal was built to accommodate the same sized boats as the Eire Canal. It was 4 feet deep, 42 feet wide at the waterline and 26 feet at the bottom. The locks were 90 feet long and 15 feet wide. It took six hours or more to travel the Canal. The expense of building the canal escalated, so to help reduce the cost they built the locks out of wood. Unfortunately the wood did not hold up and in 1848 the locks of necessity were replaced with stone. Shortly after the canal opened, mill owners found that their water flow decreased. To correct this lack of water, the upper level of the Canal was dug two and a half feet deeper. The dam was reconstructed four feet above the bottom level and a feeder was constructed from the Outlet into the Canal.

In 1853 the Canal was improved between the foot of the Lake and the village making it possible for steamboats to travel the Canal. The access to larger markets that the canal provided was a boom to the village's economy. Though the Canal was important to Penn Yan it never made money. The state stopped operating the canal in 1875. However local citizens kept it going until 1877.

The canal brought in more than $10,000 in toll revenue. What was shipped on the Canal? Lumber, timber, firewood, shingles, butter, wool, flour, wheat, rye, corn, barley, oats, peas, beans, potatoes, spirits, barley malt, fruit, furniture, castings, baskets and more were shipped out of Penn Yan. The village also benefited from what was shipped into the village. Items such as pig iron, bloom and bar iron, cuttings and iron ware, nails, spikes, horseshoes, enamelware, crockery, coal, gypsum, limestone, salt and more. Transportation by rail expanded this even further. Penn Yan's first railroad came in 1850, the Canaindaigua & Elmira Railroad

In 1884 the **Penn Yan and New York Railway** was incorporated. A group of mill owners: Calvin Russel, William Fox, Oliver G. Shearman, Seneca L. Pratt, Perley Curtiss and John T. Andrews purchased the canal from the state. A new bridge was built at Main Street to let the new railroad through. The mills in Penn Yan were raised and moved back 17 feet so they would be at street level. The new railroad terminated near the foot of Keuka Lake. Commonly called the Fall Brook Railroad, it finally merged with the New York Central Railroad. There were stations at Dresden, Cascade Mills, Mays Mills, Seneca Mills, Milo Mills, Keuka Mills and Penn Yan.

Village Incorporates. 1833 was the year the village incorporated. The space between buildings at the north and south ends of Main Street was much less than it had been. Businesses wanted to be near the Canal. Brick buildings were being built. At this time Penn Yan had a population of 1500 with 450 homes.

Fires destroyed wood buildings quickly. Before the village was incorporated in 1833 and for a while afterwards, fires were fought with a hand pump engine and buckets. At first, each property owner had a fire bucket. When a fire occurred all the males grabbed their buckets and ran creating a bucket brigade to put out the fire. The village then purchased the "Cataract" - a pump engine. It had very little power, but was better than a bucket brigade. In 1835, after the old Court House burned, Fire Engine Company Number One was established. A new brake and suction engine called the "Neptune" was purchased. It was used in the 1836 fire that burned the buildings on Brimstone Row. The Neptune was kept in a building on the north side of Elm Street where the Shearman House, which later became the Elmwood Theater, was once located. The old hand engine was kept in a small wood structure on the south side of Head Street. The fire on Brimstone Row took out the whole row of buildings on the west side of Main Street north of Elm Street – a merchant, a shoe store, a saddler, a hatter, a tailor, a physician, a druggist, two grocers, a market, and a dwelling. In 1851 the Keuka Number 1 Fire Company was organized.

In 1853 there was a fire at the corner of Main and Canal Streets in a clothing store. The fire burned north to the Tunnicliff Building, a large brick building on the corner of Main and Jacob streets (today's East Elm), and east on Canal Street. The stores that burned included those of Amasa Tuell, W. H. Watson, Edgar Sheldon, Nate

Penn Yan Fire Department's 1855 Excelsior No. 2, a Brake and Suction type engine, built by Wright Brothers of Rochester N.Y. The long poles fold down and lock to allow 6 men per side to raise and lower the poles in a teeter-totter fashion. This drove a 2 cylinder water pump to draw water from a hydrant, pond or hand filled portable water tank and provide pressure to a fire hose and nozzle. (GRL)

Madden, along with the Owls Nest. In 1855 Excelsior Number 2 Fire Company was formed. A fire station on Main Street was built and another engine was acquired. In 1857 the American Hotel on Main Street burned while the firemen were having an excursion to Hammondsport. In 1867 the Curtiss chair factory burned. It was located where St. Mark's Episcopal Church is today.

A fire house was built on Main Street near Head Street in 1858 and Excelsior Number 2 was moved there. There were three fire companies that took care of Penn Yan until 1872 when a steam fire engine called the "Keuka" was purchased. It was then that the Keuka Engine Company was organized. It later became the Ellsworth Hose Company.

In April 1872 the "Great Fire" destroyed two blocks, two hotels, thirteen dwellings, over fifty buildings and almost fifty acres all in just over two hours. The fire began in the Commercial Iron Works located on Jacob Street (now East Elm Street) where the Masonic Temple is located today. The Commercial Iron Works manufactured steam engines and boilers, shafting, pulleys and gearing, veneer cutters and chippers, plows, threshing machines and more. With a strong south wind the fire spread quickly. Firemen discovered that there was a shortage of water and telegraphed the Canandaigua and Elmira fire companies for assistance. Canandaigua came with a steam engine on a special train furnished by the Northern Central Railroad, and arrived just in time to help subdue the flames. Elmira turned around before they reached Penn Yan because they learned the fire was under control.

With help from Canandaigua, Keuka Number 1 was able to stand at the entrance to Jacob Street (now East Elm) to protect Main Street stores while Excelsior Number 2 stayed at the Benham House (located where the Community Bank is today) to protect it. The "Great Fire" destroyed the Central House, located where the Once Again Shop is today, along with its barn. The barns and outhouses of F. E. Smith and those of Nelson Thompson, the proprietor of the Benham House, were also destroyed. But, the Benham House and Main Street were saved. Damage was estimated to be approximately $130,000. In today's dollars, using production worker compensation value, that would be equivalent to $29,400,000. The gas in the pipes under the street was shut off. The streets and stores were dark that night, as if in mourning for the village's great loss. There have been many significant fires in Penn Yan. We have only touched on a few of them.

Steamboats. In 1835 the first steamboat, the *Keuka* (1835-1845), provided service on the Lake. It was owned by the Crooked Lake Steamboat Company. Built in Hammondsport, she had twin hulls, was 80 feet long and 12 feet wide, and had a five foot wide paddle wheel. She traveled back and forth from Hammondsport to Penn Yan. Because of her shallow draft she was able to run her bow into the shore, put down gangplanks and load passengers, farm animals and cargo. She was even used for celebrations. On the fourth of July her deck was used as a dance floor.

Steamboats also served Branchport. The steamer *Steuben* (1845-1864) was launched in 1845. She was 132 feet long and had a beam of 19 and a half feet. Both boats shared the Lake until the end of 1845 when the *Keuka* was taken out of service. In 1850 the *Keuka* ran aground near Hammondsport. She was towed north to Penn Yan and there was converted into the "Ark". The Ark was finally moored near a sulphur spring where it was an attraction for picnics and recreation. Another *Keuka* (1867-1875)was built. The *Steuben* burned in 1864.

Many steamboat landings appeared on Keuka Lake. Not only were there steamboats, but sailboats pulling barges also traveled the Lake. In 1864 the *George R. Youngs* (1864-1871) was built. Her name was changed to the *Steuben II* (1871-1879) in 1871 by new owners. The *Lulu* (1878-1896) and the *Yates* (1872-1883) were both built in 1870's.

The *Urbana* (1880-1904) sailed the lake in 1880. Large and fast, she set a new speed record from Hammondsport to Penn Yan with ten stops in just an hour and ten minutes. Then in 1883 came the *Holmes* (1883-1904) and the *West Branch* (1883-1902). The *Holmes* carried 63,161 passengers in the season of 1886.

Steamboats. The Steamboat *Steuben* which has pulled up at a dock along the shore of Keuka Lake. Notice the passengers on the covered upper deck of the steamboat *Mary Bell* in the lower photo. (YCGHS)

On her biggest day, August 26, 1886 she carried 1,852 passengers. On her largest single trip she transported 650 passengers from Hammondsport to Penn Yan. She ended up carrying 432,137 paying customers during her nine seasons on the lake. The passenger fare on the lake was $1.00 in 1872 and dropped down to only 10 cents in 1883. Grapes were carried for 3 cents per 100 pounds.

The *Mary Bell* (1892-1905) was a large boat; built in 1892, she could carry 600 passengers. Her name was changed to the *Penn Yan* (1905-1922) in 1905 and she was retired in 1922.

In 1895 there were seven steamboats on the Lake. In addition to the above mentioned steamboats, there was also the *Halsey* (1887-1904) whose name was changed to the *Steuben* in 1904. Another *Steuben*, *Steuben III* (1904-1915), the *Cricket* (1894-1909) and another *Yates* (1904-1915) also sailed the lake. In 1915 gasoline engines became more popular than steam. Steamboat service ended in 1922.

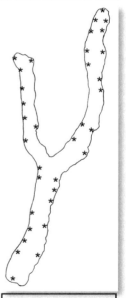

This map shows the many **steamboat landings** around Keuka Lake (SUL)

At a meeting at the American Hotel in 1840 the Yates County **Agricultural Society** was organized. The State Agricultural

Yates County Fair Grounds. The race track at the Yates County Fair when it was located where the Plaza is today on Lake Street. (YCGHS)

A Race at the County Fair. The crowd is cheering on their favorite horse and driver as they race around the track at the County Fair. (YCGHS)

Society had been founded nine years earlier in 1831. The Yates County Society had 140 members. They held their first fair at the Court House park a few months later and continued the fair there until 1851. Exhibits were located inside.

The fair moved to Dundee for two years. Then in 1853 four acres were set aside on what is now Keuka Street. The land was fenced and a hall was built. In 1871 the Society purchased 18 acres on Lake Street where the Lake Street Plaza is located today. There they built a half mile race track used for horse races. At the 1899 fair there was a race between a horse and a "horseless carriage." This was also the year that a silver cup was awarded to the winner of the championship bicycle race.

In 1901 Carrie Nation appeared at the fair with her hatchet in one hand and her bible in the other. She was a radical member of the temperance movement and believed that if she destroyed enough saloons she could stop the evil of alcohol. She would enter a saloon with her hatchet and bible and attack the bar. They say she attracted 4,000 people to the fair. At the 1931 fair it was the Evangelist Billy Sunday that assured everyone that they could be saved. Robert Ingersoll also spoke at the fair.

The fair was a huge attraction; residents looked forward to it each year. The village was expanding around the fair grounds. So the Society's officers decided to sell the grounds on Lake Street and move. The Fair Grounds were sold in 1952 and the fair moved to land near the Penn Yan Airport. In 1960 the current fair ground was purchased. The Yates County Fair is one of the oldest in New York State.

In **1848** the canal's wooden locks were replaced with those made of stone. This was also the year that a plank road was planned going

Northern Central Depot. This post-card shows one of the old depots in Penn Yan. It was located at E. Elm & Hamilton streets. (YCGHS)

The Fall Brook Rail Way. Here you can see the tracks along the Outlet looking towards Main Street. (TPC)

The Train. Trains brought faster transportation to the region for both people and cargo. (YCGHS)

from Dresden to Penn Yan but was not built until 1852. Plans were underway for a railroad to travel from Corning through Penn Yan and on to Canandaigua. Steamboats traveled the lakes providing transportation for both people and cargo.

A **railroad** finally arrived in 1850. The Canandaigua and Elmira Railway was the first in the village. It later became the Northern Central. Still later it was part of the Pennsylvania Railroad. As previously mentioned, in 1884 another railroad ran along the Canal a few years after it closed. Transportation became even easier and goods could reach the outside world faster. With lake transportation between Penn Yan and Hammondsport, people and cargo could reach Bath and then the Erie and Lackawana Rail Road. Businesses expanded. Penn Yan had an active grain and produce market and many goods were now manufactured and grown here.

The **1850s** brought hotels, boarding houses, women owned businesses, a female academy, the founding of the co-educational institution – Penn Yan Academy, two newspapers and much more. Women were fighting for their rights in Seneca Falls. There was a **Woman's Rights Convention** in Penn Yan in 1855. It was held at the Methodist Meeting House with Susan B. Anthony and Ernestine L. Rose as speakers. There were seven churches, some of which were the result of the split among Protestant churches over disagreements among their congregations relating to the abolition of slavery. Former New Englanders tended to support abolition. The County had a small black population. An escaped slave, William Maxfield, was a canal-boatman. He hid slaves in casks on the dock. Another former runaway slave, John Thomas, ran an Underground Railroad station from his home on Jackson Street (now Linden Street). Merchant Henry Bradley's house was a station on the **Underground Railroad** as well. He ran for Governor of New York in 1846 as an abolitionist.

There were 3000 people living in Penn Yan in 1855. Penn Yan's population came from all over. There were immigrants from Ireland, England, Scotland, Canada, Bavaria, Germany, Switzerland and France. There were nine grocery stores, fourteen general stores, two hardware stores, four shoe stores, two banks, two livery stables and an iron foundry. It was also at this time that Yates County had a higher yield of winter wheat per acre than any other county in the country. Too much wheat led to a reduction in price. In 1857 banks found they did not have enough gold reserves for their obligations and a severe depression struck the nation. A run on the Yates County Bank caused it to fail. Lincoln won the Presidency in November 1860 with the enthusiastic support of Penn Yan residents. War was on the horizon.

The Mills. This image shows Penn Yan's milling section. At one time Penn Yan had a large number of businesses producing many different types of goods. (YCGHS)

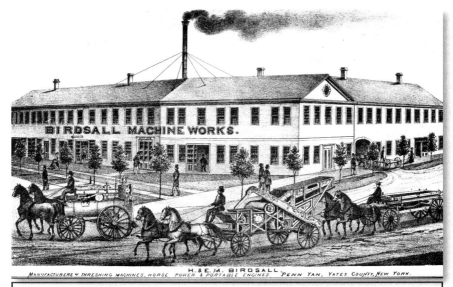

Birdsall Machine Works. This image is from the 1876 Yates County Atlas. Birdsall was located at Head and Main streets and built farm equipment.

The Penn Yan Gas Light Company was organized in 1860. The plant was located on Jackson Street. It provided light for Penn Yan. H. Birdsall & Son became a Penn Yan business in 1860. They built threshers and other equipment. Later they produced and repaired steam engines for steamboats. Many businesses were created or expanded as a result of the Canal and better transportation.

Before the war the Keuka Outlet had a dozen dams and at its peak as many as 40 **mills** were powered by its water. They consisted of grist and sawmills, carding machines, fulling mills, tanneries, plaster mills, distilleries, woolen and cotton factories, spoke factories, shingle mills, trip-hammers and more. There were also paper mills. Paper was produced mainly from straw pulp.

South Carolina seceded from the Union in December 1860. The nation was on the brink of **Civil War**. Fort Sumter fell and on April 15, 1861 and Lincoln called for 75,000 volunteers. In May the "Keuka Rifles", a company of the 33rd New York, became the first group of local men to join the Union forces. There was a ceremony at the Court House and a parade to the railroad station. At that time most people thought the war would end quickly. As the war continued Lincoln called for a draft. Another 572 Yates County men were drafted. More men left leaving their families to fend for themselves. Once they were allowed even the village's black men joined up. One, Thomas

Jefferson VanHouten, enlisted early in the 54th Massachusetts, the Union's 1st "colored" regiment. 2,109 Yates County men served in the Civil War. That was over 10% of the local population, about 40% of those eligible.

Grape Picking. The vineyard's harvest is being picked by hand as it was in the past. (YCGHS)

Grapes were beginning to become a major crop. Though there were wild grapes here when the first settlers arrived, they were not cultivated until years later. The industry started about 1836. It wasn't until the 1840s that grapes were shipped to larger cities in any significant quantity.

In 1858 table grapes were selling for as much as 35 cents per pound. Grapes for wine were only 18 cents per pound. Isabellas and Concords were grown on the hillsides in the 1860s. Vineyards expanded significantly during the period of 1865 to 1870. Factories produced unfermented grape juice. The Seneca Lake Grape and Wine Company, with 125 acres in Milo, had the largest vineyard in New York State.

With so many grapes being grown, baskets for picking and shipping were needed. In 1866 the Hopkins Brothers opened the first basket factory in Penn Yan, located off Main Street behind where the Library sits today. In 1914 a newspaper article reported that Penn Yan led New York State in basket making. It was estimated that 50 million baskets were shipped out of Penn Yan that year. The three

Lake Keuka grapes for N.Y. markets (YCGHS)

largest factories at that time were: Guile and Windnagle's, Yates Lumber Company, both located on the south side of the Outlet east of Liberty Street, and Barden and Robeson's, located on Head Street. The first baskets made were for berries. Basket manufacturers made

The Half-Bushel Climax Basket

THE use of this package is increasing every year. It is fast taking the place of trays and boxes in the shipping of tray grapes, and is one of the most popular packages in use.

The Four Pound Climax

This package is used principally for grapes. Great care is taken to have the material of selected white. It is unequaled in strength and appearance.

Climax Basket. Images of the half-bushel and the four pound Climax baskets from a Yates Lumber Company catalogue. There is no date on the catalogue. It depicts baskets of many different sizes for different types of fruit.

Peach baskets are also shown in the catalog. It has been said that Mr. Potter was selling baskets at Springfield, Massachusetts when Jim Naismith asked for a peach basket to try for a new sport he was developing – basketball. (BSC)

grape baskets, peach baskets, picking baskets, market baskets, clothes baskets, bamboo and splint delivery baskets, satchel lunch baskets and more. As we have mentioned earlier, steamboat service on the lake expanded to serve the grape industry. They were able to stop at many docks along the Lake where they could pick up

Yates Lumber Company. This image of Yates Lumber Company and Basket Factory is from their catalogue of baskets. (BSC)

Wise Fruit House. William Wise, "the grape king" stored, packed and shipped fruit. This is his fruit house. Note the rail tracks which went past the warehouse to the ice house. Railroad cars were loaded with fruit and ice which was cut from Keuka Lake in the winter and saved till fall. (YCGHS)

Empire State Winery. This image is from the 1930s. The building was built in 1896. This building was located on Lake Street on the vacant lot which now sits between Knapp & Schlappi and the Perri's Boat Yard Grill (formerly Sarrasin's Restaurant.) The cupola can still be seen sitting today next to some brush. (YCGHS)

Empire State Wine vineyards postcard (TPC)

Packing Grapes. In this image we see women and children gathered around a table putting grapes into baskets. (YCGHS)

grapes to take to Hammondsport and to Penn Yan for further shipping on the Canal or by train.

In 1916 "the grape king", William N. Wise, reported that it had been an exceptional year for grapes. Delawares were selling for $80 to $85 per ton. Catawbas sold for $65 per ton. They had sold the year before at $35 to $45 per ton. Concords also sold in bulk rather than baskets. The harvest was completely sold four

Grape Labels. Two grape labels which would have appeared on baskets of grapes. Samuel McMath packed and shipped table grapes. They were shipped by train to cities on the northeast. The Lake Keuka Fruit Exchange label was used by grape packers who did not have their own label. (YCGHS)

weeks early. In 1919, 1407 train cars filled with grapes were shipped out of the Central New York lake section. 1920 was another good year for grapes. Concords sold at $115 per ton; Catawbas sold for $100 per ton. Some grapes sold for $140 per ton. It was also in 1920 that the Finger Lakes district was called the "Rhineland of America" by a Federal agency. When describing the grape growing district of the Finger Lakes, they said it was one of most interesting grape growing regions of the country.

Wineries. The first winery in the area was erected in 1870 – the Seneca Lake Wine Company. In 1860 newspaper editor Stafford

Cleveland wrote an editorial about the prohibition of alcohol. Of course, whiskey had been distilled in the town ever since the first settlers arrived. It wasn't until 1874 that the Women's Christian Temperance Union was formed in Penn Yan. Still in 1894 the Village Directory reported six wineries: Barney Borgman's – on Elm Street, Empire State Winery – on Seneca Street, Hammondsport Vintage Company – on Seneca Street, TSB Wine Company – at Jacob and Seneca Streets and Seneca Lake Wine Company – on Seneca Street. G. C. and W. C. Snow made unfermented grape juice. The Empire State Wine Company was organized by A. Clinton Brooks and Frank Hallett. They had a first class laboratory supplied with French, German and American instruments for use for chemical analysis of wines and the soils used for growing grapes. The winery owned vineyards on Bluff Point and had their own steamboat dock as well as a private switch on the Fall Brook Rail Road. They won medals for their wine. They had a beautiful stone building on Lake Street just south of where Knapp & Schlappi is located today.

The *Parsons Penn Yan, Dundee & Yates County Directory* for **1892** showed that Penn Yan had 20 societies. Penn Yan's population was very active. There were 4 newspapers: the Yates County Chronicle, the Penn Yan Express, and the Penn Yan Democrat were all weeklies. The Vineyardist came out semi-monthly. The Fall Brook Railway and the Northern Central Railway were the two railroads. There were 5 boarding houses, 3 book and stationery stores, 6 boot and shoe stores, 2 bottlers, 6 carriage manufacturers and dealers, 5 cigar manufacturers and dealers, 6 clothiers and gents furnishing stores, 27 dressmakers, 4 druggists, 5 dry goods stores, 2 fruit evaporators, 16 grocers, 5 hardware stores, 11 hotels, 13 lawyers, 3 livery stables, 9 meat markets, 6 milliners, 14 physicians, 6 produce dealers, 5 printers, 7 restaurants, 7 saloons, 3 variety stores, and 3 wine and brandy manufacturers. Of course there were still other businesses I have not listed.

In 1894 there were 26 vineyards listed in the County's directory. In 1909 Yates County became the **first all dry county in New York State**. Local prohibition had quite an effect on grape production. It was cut in half. Some vineyards were replanted into table and juice grapes. Paul Garrett, who had 4,000 acres in this area along with processing plants, was able to survive by making other products and juice with his grapes. The Garrett Company made non-intoxicating wine and extracts. People were allowed to make wine in their homes for personal consumption. Salesmen taught people how to turn grape juice into wine for personal use. Some even returned to help their customers bottle the "juice". There were more than 2500 commercial wineries in the United States before prohibition and less than 100 afterwards.

Temperance and suffrage were both strong movements. In 1913 the Political Equality Club was formed as a part of the New York State suffrage movement. In 1915 the Yates County Men's League for Women Suffrage was formed. Despite this, when the the referendum first came to a vote it was defeated. Women did not gain the right to vote until 1920 and that was primarily due to their contribution during the war. The 18th Amendment prohibiting alcohol was passed in 1919, but did not take effect till 1920. The local paper reported that in the days before the amendment went into effect local wineries were practically giving away their wine. People came from Rochester to purchase alcohol in Penn Yan. There were even special buses from Geneva. The wine stock quickly disappeared. Prohibition did not end until December 1933.

Tourism Industry. In 1875 the tourism industry began in earnest in Penn Yan. Trees were planted and old fences were removed to make the village more attractive for summer visitors and the Court House and Academy yards were turned into parks. Visitors could rent small cottages along Keuka Lake in Jerusalem.

Crystal Spring resort was built in Barrington in 1864. It was a destination for the healing powers of spring water, bringing people from as far away as Philadelphia and Washington, DC. The first Crystal Spring hotel was built in 1866. Hotels were located there through 1905. Grove Springs House opened along the Lake in Wayne in 1869. That was also the year that the Keuka Yacht Club was organized.

Crystal Spring House. This picture shows the Crystal Spring House after it was enlarged in 1867. It was 42 feet wide and 100 feet long, with about 70 apartments along with dining rooms, parlors and public rooms. There was also a separate bath house containing 12 rooms each with a tub – 6 for women and 6 for men. Hot and cold spring water was piped into each room. The resort also contained a recreation building where guests could dance or play billiards. It was estimated that 5,000 people attended the grand opening in July 1868. (DAHS)

Giant fish catch about 1919, possibly at the Gibson House at Gibson's Landing (YCGHS)

Grove Springs House. Grove Springs House was located in Wayne. It was a popular vacation spot on Keuka Lake, about 12 miles south of Penn Yan in the town of Wayne. People came from New York City, Baltimore and Washington D.C. (YCGHS)

In 1880 the Grove Springs House was improved. When it burned in 1915 it had the capacity for 100 guests. A favorite outing for guests was taking a carriage to Eggleston's Gully to hike to the beautiful 100 foot falls.

Several hotels opened near the lake providing destinations for summer vacations. Visitors enjoyed boating, fishing, picnicking, music, swimming and many of the same activities summer visitors do today. They were able to travel to the area by train, carriages and of course automobiles. Escaping from the heat of the cities was a great relief.

The "Ark" located near Red Jacket Park was a popular attraction. It was created in 1850 when the steamboat *Keuka* ran aground in Hammondsport. She

A Cottage at Keuka Lake, a fairly typical cottage of the late 1800s along Keuka Lake. (YCGHS)

Golfing at Lakeside Country Club in 1940. It opened as a 9 hole course in 1923, expanded to 18 holes in 1995. A new clubhouse was built in 1987. (TH/PYK)

Boating on Keuka, a favorite pastime during the summer was boating on the Lake. (YCGHS).

was towed to Penn Yan and beached; anything worth salvaging was taken off and what was left was purchased by Calvin Carpenter for $25. He placed her cabins on a scow. His wife thought the new craft looked like an ark, so it was called the Ark from that time on. Carpenter made ginger ale which visitors enjoyed along with other refreshments. In 1873 he built a new Ark. In 1880 D. Edward Dewey from Canandaigua purchased the Ark and located it next door to a sulphur spring where people came to get water. It was also popular for Dewey's lemon beer. It wasn't just the locals who went to the Ark, people arrived by coach from the train station. In 1904 it was demolished and the site was used for a number of summer cottages. Penn Yan had restaurants, hotels, saloons, pool halls

The Ark. Here you see an image of the second Ark. It was a popular attraction in the late 1800s. (YCGHS)

and bowling alleys to serve tourists and residents. P. T. Barnum's circus came to town in 1873 for a show that drew huge crowds. Tourism was to become popular in the whole Finger Lakes region.

Cottages and summer homes were being built along Keuka Lake. They were used mainly in July and August. In 1905 one of the first camps for children opened at Eggleston's Point, Camp Arey. In 1921 the YMCA's Camp Cory opened on 13 acres on the east side of Keuka Lake. A survey of the number of automobiles in Yates County conducted in June 1921 showed 2,666. To put this in perspective, Penn Yan had a population of 4517 in 1920.

The Finger Lakes Association promoted the area. They put up three 8 by 12 foot signs promoting Keuka. Here

Fishing. Vacationers had many activities at the Lake. So did those who lived in Penn Yan. Here you see two fishermen proudly displaying their catch. Keuka was known for its supply of good fish. (YCGHS)

is some of the copy – all three signs began with "Red Jacket Trail to Lake Keuka". Then the copy was different on each sign. "The most beautiful of All the Finger Lakes. Penn Yan, (Lake Keuka), 17 miles, Watkins Glen, 42 miles, Elmira, 67 miles, New York, 316 miles." appeared on a sign in Flint. Two others had the following copy: "Lake Keuka, the Home of the Senecas. The most influential tribe of the Confederacy. Red Jacket and Corn Planter were prominent chieftains of this clan." and "In 1795 Louis Phillipe, later King of France, was guest of the Public Universal Friend, and spent much of his time hunting and fishing in this locality." In 1923 the state decided to open a park on the Bluff as a part of a Finger Lakes park system. It was to be on property owned by William T. Morris. The depression resulted in those plans being set aside. The current Keuka State Park did not open until 1964. The site was selected in 1961. The state had also considered Camp Arey on the east leg of the Lake.

A Tour Guide. As early as 1927 the Finger Lakes Association of Central New York was promoting the beauty of the area. This shows the cover of their booklet and one of the pages focused on Keuka Lake. (YCGHS).

In 1927 a booklet titled "The Beautiful Finger Lakes Call You." was put out by the Finger Lakes Association of Central New York. The copy about Penn Yan included the following: "Penn Yan, from the time it was settled in 1799, has been a town of real progress. In 1823 it was made the county seat of Yates County and today it is the hub of one of the richest farming areas in the lake country. It is the turning point in the majestic lakeshore drive to Hammondsport and it is the door to the motoring thrills that abound in a spin

Ball Hall as it was when Keuka College was first built. Dr. and Mrs. Ball can be seen at the top of the steps. (TPC)

out to the end of Bluff Point, 'The Crows-nest of the Finger Lakes'." By 1935 the Directory of the Owners of Cottages and Lake Front Homes on Keuka Lake listed 1192 addresses. There were 649 on the Penn Yan branch and 228 on the Branchport branch. This area was even then considered to be a very special place.

In 1890 Penn Yan's population was 4254. That was the year that **Keuka College** was formed. Located on the shore of Keuka Lake between Penn Yan and Branchport it was a coeducational institution with a farm, a dairy barn, a basket factory and their own water works. A brochure put out in 1891 stated that Keuka College was "pre-eminently, for the common people.. with ample endowment ... it will raise an army of country people from comparative ignorance and consequent weakness to superior men and women who shall bring strength to the nation and help to humanity." The college closed in 1915 due to lack of funds. In 1917 there was a proposal to make it a training camp for soldiers but that never came to be. The Baptists began a fund raising effort so that the college could be reopened. They were looking to raise $333,000. The college opened again in 1921, this time as a college for women. In 1985 it became coeducational again.

Farming. Farmers hard at work and farms as they were many years ago. This region is still known for its farmland and its hard working farmers. (All farming images from YCGHS)

By the 1890's **farming** was becoming a big business. Machinery improved and fertilizers resulted in better crops. In 1874, two hundred thousand bushels of apples were grown on 2242 farms. In a single week, Charles Hunter & Company shipped 84 tons of grapes, peaches, pears and apples. Over 560,000 bushels of corn was produced. In 1889, four farmers raised three thousand pounds of tobacco. In the 1880s came the first large scale evaporation (or drying) of fruit. Shipping fresh fruit led to the need for ice houses and many picking and packing containers. As Penn Yan slipped into the twentieth century prices went up. New products were coming into favor – beans, cabbage, peas, dried fruit. Dairy farming in this area became popular in the 1920s. With better technology farm production increased and the number of farmers decreased. Opportunities for people to work off the farm also increased. The mechanization of farming meant that land was easier to farm if it was flat. Many of the farms around Penn Yan were hilly. Prices were good during World War 1. Afterwards they went down. Farmers had to borrow money and many were not able to pay it back. In the 1920's a national farm depression resulted in 1 in 4 farms being sold to meet financial obligations.

Wagener Brothers Shoes was a very successful company. This shows their second factory which was located on Seneca Street. (YCGHS)

Walker Bin Factory made special display bins with glass fronts and beautiful wood work for homes and churches. (YCGHS)

Manufacturing continued to grow. Paper, baskets, agricultural machinery and tools, paper making machinery, blinds and doors, wheel spokes and hubs, malt, wine, vinegar, cider and woven wire for fences were all produced in Penn Yan. There was also grain, lumber, fresh fruits and dried fruits. Services expanded as well. W. H. Whitfield was established in 1872. They made fine carriages and harnesses. Whitfield's son Charles joined the business and they created the "Peerless" grape wagon. It was able to hold 1000 baskets and transport them without damaging their fragile cargo. Wheels and spokes were manufactured in a mill on the Outlet in 1875. Penn Yan Wheel Company bought the business in 1880 and made complete wheels. Then in 1890 A. J. Dibble purchased the factory and the name became the Dibble Spoke Company.

Barden & Robeson had a plant off Head Street in 1909 making high quality baskets. Seneca Mills replaced Yates Company Oil Mill on the Outlet in 1884, converting the mill into a paper mill. They made news print and book paper. It was later leased out to a company that made high quality white and fibre papers from straw. The latter was not successful so the mill was dismantled and beginning about 1889 Seneca Mill produced electric power for Penn Yan. The water rights were later acquired by Yates Electrical Light and Power Company. Eventually NYSEG took over. The mill was finally razed in 1958.

The Wagener Brothers Shoe Company was organized in 1900 in a building located behind Sheppard's Opera House. In 1902 they built a new plant on Seneca Street at Central Avenue. It was sold in 1911 to the Rochester Shoe Company.

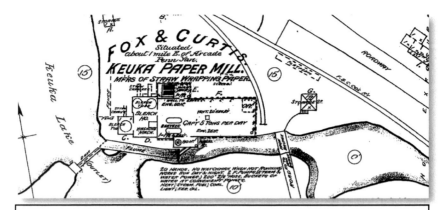

Sanborn Map. This image is from the 1886 Sanborn Map of Penn Yan and vicinity. Sanborn maps were made to provide insurance companies with information about all the properties located in a particular town to help them assess risk. This particular image is of the Fox – Curtiss Paper Mill.

Fox's Paper Mill on the Outlet. They made paper out of straw pulp from 1865 to 1945. (YCGHS)

In 1907 George Frederick started a small canning factory that canned apples and plums under the name of the Yates County Canning Company. In 1913 it was a large factory canning all kinds of fruit berries, beans and tomatoes.

In 1906 the Yates Lumber Company took over the Potter Lumber Company and renamed it. In 1909 they added the manufacture of Climax Baskets for grapes and other fruits. In 1911 they sold 5,800,000 baskets. The Combination Vender Company began business in 1906 manufacturing a four compartment vending machine. The Penn Yan Cable Company, located in front of the Wagener Brothers Shoe factory, made electrical conduits and conductors. In 1909, the Walker Bin Company produced a tilting, pivoted bin mounted in a bin chamber so that it could operate on its own. The bin had a glass front so that the merchandise inside could be seen. It was popular in grocery and seed stores. You can see one today at Knapp & Schlappi Lumber Company on Lake Street.

In the years to come still more manufacturing jobs became available with the arrival of Michaels Stern, Penn Yan Boats, and Whitfield & Sons' move from making carriages to building bus bodies.

In 1922 the payroll for manufacturing in Penn Yan totaled one million dollars. The businesses who reported their payroll included: Walker Bin Company, Guile and Windnagle, Empire State Wine Company, Whitfield and Son, Barden and Robeson, Yates Canning Company, Penn Yan Boat Company, Taylor Chemical Company, Andrews Brothers, Birkett Mills, Fox Mills, Michaels Stern, Niagara Wall Board, Milo Ribbon and Carbon, Yates Electric Light, Short Electric Company and Cramer Brothers.

Trolley Route. A segment from the 1899 Yates County map which shows the trolley route from Penn Yan to Branchport and back. (YCH)

The Trolley at the four corners of Elm Street, East Elm and Main. On the left you can see Wheeler's Drugs which later became Bordwell's Drugs. You can also see 101 Main Street on the right side of the image – now the location of Goin' Postal. The trolley was only permitted to travel at a speed of 20 miles per hour so that it would not scare horses. Note the horse and carriage in the picture. (YCGHS)

Trolley Service. In 1897 trolley service came to Penn Yan when the Penn Yan, Keuka Park & Branchport Railway was built. Nicknamed the "Toonerville Trolley" it was powered by electricity. The route was 8 miles long with a power station near Keuka Park at the half way point where the car barns were also located. Fares were 15 cents one way and 25 cents round trip. When it had been in operation only a year passenger traffic amounted to 100,000 fares. One Sunday it carried 2000 passengers. It also carried freight. In fact, during the first 20 days it was in operation the trolley carried two million pounds of freight. Freight stations were located in Branchport, Kinney's Corners and at Park Landing.

Electric Park. The trolley had an electric station and car barn at about the half way point of their route. It was located along the lake and became a popular picnic place. There were public docks, refreshments were available and there was a dance pavilion. This image shows the park. When the trolley stopped service cottages were built here. (YCGHS)

The trolley's power station, called Electric Park, soon became a popular picnic area. Later a dance pavilion was located there. The trolley and steamboats worked together for a special excursion. Passengers could board a steamboat in Penn Yan at 2:30 p.m. and travel around the bluff to the west branch of Keuka Lake. They would arrive in Branchport at 5:00 p.m. having enjoyed the scenery along the east and west branches of Keuka Lake. Then they could spend

Penn Yan in 1908. This is an image of Main Street during a carnival in 1908. You can see the trolley tracks in the foreground. Streets were still dirt. (YCGHS)

some time picnicking or exploring Branchport and catch the trolley back to Penn Yan. The trolley had departures from Branchport at 5:10, 6:10, 7:00, 7:50, 8:40 and 9:30 p.m.. The trip took just 40 minutes. Passengers rode along the Lake through farms and past Keuka College and the Keuka Yacht Club. All this for just 30 cents.

In 1926 the trolley announced that it would no longer be providing passenger service. Because of the automobile and bus service it was no longer profitable. Yet that winter they reinstituted service. Finally in March 1927 all passenger service stopped. Freight service ended in 1928. They were not the only transportation service having difficulties. The Pennsylvania Rail Road announced that passenger trains 8415 and 8416 between Elmira and Canandaigua would no longer run effective January 1926. The trolley tracks were removed in 1936 as part of a WPA project. The trolley had been a great convenience to the people who built summer homes along the Lake as well as the students at Keuka College.

By **1899** Penn Yan had 9 meat markets, 13 grocers, 3 bottling works, 8 barbers, 17 dressmakers, 3 laundries, 6 cigar makers, 10 saloons, 9 hotels, 6 boarding houses, 9 insurance agencies, 5 music teachers, 4 photographers, 7 harness makers, and 4 livery stables. In 1902 telephone service came to Penn Yan.

The arrival of the automobile. The first large scale production of the automobile in the United States began in 1902 with the Olds Motor Vehicle Company. The first person to own a car in this area is said to have been Dr. A. T. Halsted of Rushville. In 1903 he owned a Maxwell. That same year Penn Yan had a place to purchase an automobile, Wagener Brothers Automobile Exchange. It was located on Jacob Street (now East Elm Street) opposite the Sampson Theatre. They were in business from 1903 through 1917 selling the National, the Haynes, Hudson, Reo and Studebaker. When the business began it sold 6 or 7 cars a year. Soon they were selling 400 new cars a year. Of course the arrival of the automobile helped the growth of the tourist industry.

Wagener Brothers Automobile Exchange which was located opposite the Sampson House Theater. The image comes from Walter Wolcott's book on Penn Yan published in 1914.

In **1905** a steam powered electric plant was built in Penn Yan. Residents were no longer dependent upon the hydropower which the Outlet provided. Public water and sewers also came to the village, all from one place where the Penn Yan water treatment plant is today.

Camp Arey. Said to be the first organized camp in the US, it was created by Professor Albert Arey and was a science camp for boys located on the west side of Canandaigua Lake in 1890. Professor Arey moved the camp to Eggleston Point on Keuka Lake in 1905. Professor Arey retired in 1915 and his daughter, Mildred ran the camp with an emphasis on sports. She turned the camp into one just for girls. The camp was sold to the Patin family in 1936. They continued to run it as a girls camp for a few more years. The property, now a manufactured home park, was once owned by John D. Rockefeller. A wheel chair was stored there in case he visited. (YCGHS)

44

The first camp came to the area in 1905 when Professor Albert Arey, who had run a Natural Science Camp on leased property at Canandaigua Lake, purchased 160 acres at Eggleston Point in Barrington about 10 miles south of Penn Yan on Keuka Lake. It was a summer school for boys where they were taught outdoor sports. It could accommodate 150 students. It was the oldest and largest natural science camp in the United States. It later became a girls camp. Still later it was purchased for a manufactured home park.

Penn Yan's population decreased in 1905 to 4504. In 1906 the first brick pavements were put down. East Elm Street was the first to be paved because salesmen did not like to get all dusty when they left the train station and the village wanted to look progressive. In July the Keuka Yacht Club held an illuminated carnival. They urged people to decorate their boats including lights. Sail and rowboats would be towed by power boats. The parade was scheduled for 8:45 p.m.. This was also the year that three women were nominated for the Penn Yan school board. This had never happened before. No women were elected for another twenty-two years and then only because the men had brought everything to a standstill.

The **new post office** site was chosen in 1909. It was to be built next to the Benham House. At that time the post office was located

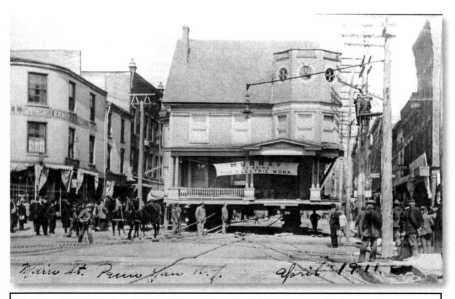

A New Post Office. In this picture from April 1911 we see the house that was located on the site for the new Post Office being moved along Main Street to make room for the new building. (YCGHS)

in the Arcade building. C. B. Struble decided if the post office was moving he would remodel the Arcade to include an opera house. He would move the telephone office to the front of the building. Then he could create seating for 600 to 700 people with 1,700 square feet. The second and third floors could be a balcony and gallery. The post office was built across the street, but the Arcade opera house never came to be.

In 1910 the Sampson Theater opened on East Elm Street. They began with vaudeville, had live local talent and then silent films. There was a roller skating rink behind the Central House.

Hatmaker's Hospital. The first hospital in Penn Yan was Susannah Hatmaker's hospital located at 246 East Main Street. This is a postcard showing what the building looked like then. Except for the lack of porches and shutters and a different front door, the exterior is essentially unchanged today. (YCGHS)

In 1911 Penn Yan got its first **hospital**. Susannah Hatmaker, R.N. opened a private hospital at 246 East Main Street. The house still stands today. It included seven rooms for patients, an operating room, administration and other rooms. All patients were under the care of a doctor. The hospital closed in 1917 when Susannah left for France as an Army Nurse.

After a terrible influenza outbreak in 1918 – 1919, which resulted in closed schools and no public gatherings, the community decided that they needed to build a larger hospital. Members of the community were already talking about a suitable memorial to those who fought in World War 1. William N. Wise organized others, plans were made and funds were raised. In 1922 the Hospital committee said they had raised enough money to build. They expected to break ground in the spring of 1922 north of North Avenue on the west side of Main Street for a 32 bed hospital dedicated to our "boys" who fought so gallantly for us and the world. The Soldiers & Sailors Memorial Hospital finally opened in October 1924.

World War I. In 1914, like many places, Penn Yan did not expect to become involved in the great war. The United States declared war on April 6, 1917. On the evening of April 19th the Home Defense Committee called a meeting outside of the Knapp House. Over 1,000

Soldiers & Sailors Memorial Hospital. A postcard showing the new hospital. It was competed in 1924. (YCGHS)

The Hospital Garage. Here you can see the hospital's garage. (YCGHS)

men, women and children attended. Stars and stripes appeared on every business and public building. The band played patriotic songs and the crowd sang led by Thomas Reynolds, the Democratic Party chairman, and William S. Cornwell, chair of the Republican party. George R. Cornwell spoke about the War not being of our choosing. Still, he called for unity and remarked that the battle should be entered and pursued in the spirit of the Rebellion (the Civil War). President Woodrow Wilson asked for help to supply the troops and our allies with food, supplies and ships. He said the "fate of the nation rests on farmers." Farmers were encouraged to increase production. Every citizen was asked to have a garden.

In June a Selective Draft required all men ages 21 to 30 to enroll. Yates County enrolled 1207. In July Yates County drafted 122 men.

Off to War. Here is a picture from September 1917 of a parade on Main Street heading toward the train station to send off young men to war. Leading the parade are veterans from the Civil War. They are just turning at the four corners of Main and Elm Streets toward the Pennsylvania Station. (YCGHS)

On September 9th 1917 the first five men departed. The four Penn Yan Fire Department companies and the Penn Yan Band organized a huge send off. At 7:00 p.m. they gathered for a parade followed by an assembly at the park. There was a short address by County Judge Gilbert H. Baker and then off to the train station. Those first five men were: Stephen A. Whitman, Thomas P. Carroll, William Finerghty, Charles E. Costello and Perl Douglass. It wasn't until April 1918 that the first soldiers made it to the front. By October 1918 Yates County had more than 500 men serving in the military.

Travel here became difficult. Traffic on the railroads and on the lake was cut off. The winter of 1917 and 1918 found the area with a shortage of coal. William N. Wise was appointed Yates County Fuel Administrator. Because of the lack of fuel, mail delivery was stopped for a while. Street lights and electric signs could only be lit on Saturday nights. On January 21, 1918, Wise announced that no fuel could be used on Mondays in any factory, business place or office, except as might be necessary to prevent injury to property from freezing with a few exceptions: transportation companies, banks, dentists and physicians, drug stores, stores where food was sold before twelve noon and coal yard offices. To help conserve fuel, garages and service stations were closed at night and on Sundays.

Concerned about local citizens who were immigrants from Germany and Denmark, as well as those from Ireland, who were not happy to be allied with the British, the sheriff posted notices reminding people to leave their neighbors alone as long as they were obeying the law. Liberty bonds were promoted. In early November 1917 Baldwins and Citizens banks reported over 1,500 bond subscribers resulting in more than $400,000. Glenn Curtiss' aircraft plant in Hammondsport had a military guard.

Newspapers had cartoons and articles supporting prohibition. Wouldn't it be better to make bread with grain rather than liquor? Of course Yates County already had prohibition, but the country did not. On December 17, 1917 the Federal government voted for national prohibition. In January 1918 President Wilson began talks with British Prime Minister David Lloyd George. These talks resulted in the fourteen points which became the basis for the German surrender.

By fall it became obvious that the war was coming to a close. News of the **Armistice** came to Penn Yan at 2:45 a.m. on November 11th. At 3:45 the fire bell rang telling people that peace was at hand. Then church bells began to ring and people began to gather in the street. There was a large bonfire in the middle of the four corners at Elm and Main Streets which was kept burning till afternoon. A parade began at 7:15 p.m. at the foot of Main Street, marching up the street to the Arcade building, on to Head Street and then back to where they started. Civil War veterans were followed by the police, village and county boards, the fire department, the New York State guard, clergymen, the Red Cross, the Scouts – both boy and girl, the Penn Yan Band and citizens carrying noise makers of every kind. At the end of the parade there were speeches made by the Reverends Boyd and Gommenginger, Edson Potter, and Orville Randolph. Nat Sackett sang the star spangled banner. All the businesses were closed that day and finally the crowd burned an effigy of the Kaiser. At last the war was over.

On July 4th Penn Yan welcomed home their local soldiers with a Welcome Home Day for Soldiers. Each man was given a bronze medal with his name engraved on it. Exercises began late morning and continued late into the evening. There was entertainment, a dinner, sports, a parade and fireworks. The people of Penn Yan were truly appreciative of the service made by their men and, oh, so proud.

In 1921 the marsh across from the Lakeview Cemetery was ceded to the village by the State for use as a park. Today the ball fields are located there.

In **1922** Penn Yan's population was 5,000. This was the year that the village instituted its first zoning laws. In 1923 George Excell operated a tourist camp opposite what is now Red Jacket Park. His home and apple orchard were located on both sides of Lake Street. Excell Tourist Camp was on the east side of the road with access to the Lake on the other side. There were cement fireplaces for travelers to cook on. People could park their travel trailers there or pitch a tent for 25 cents per night. Later he added an amusement area with archery, horseshoes, shuffleboard and even miniature golf. Refreshments were also available for purchase. Across the street there were steps leading down the bank to the Lake. The bank itself was covered with poison ivy. People came from all over to stay there. George Excell would later sell the lakefront property to the village for very little money so that it could be made into a public park. The village held a contest to name the park and "Red Jacket" was the winner. Excell's Tourist Camp remained in business until he retired in 1954.

Roads. In 1923 people were interested in building a road along the east side of Keuka Lake from Penn Yan to Hammondsport. Improvements were being made on the dirt road on the west side of the Lake. In 1922 they paved the road from Hammondsport to Urbana; in 1923 and 1924 they paved the section from Urbana to Pulteney Landing. Finally during 1924 and 1925 they paved the section from Pulteney Landing to the Yates County line. In 1931 Steuben County paved the road from Hammondsport along the east side of the Lake up to the Yates County line. In 1932 the road was extended to Crosby. Concrete resulted in much safer roads than dirt.

In **1927** Penn Yan had 18 auto dealers, garages, repairers and supplies, 23 grocers, 17 insurance agents, 11 lawyers, 2 banks, 14 physicians, 2 newspapers, 3 railways and so much more.

In 1928 the State Board of Education told the village that they had serious concerns about the condition and size of Penn Yan's schools. It was true – they were both over crowded and in very poor condition. Highways were improved so that travel into the country was even easier. There were good years after the war, but they were about to come to an end. **The Crash of 1929** and the resulting depression had an effect on everyone. If you read the papers of Penn Yan during that time you would not see great devastation. But, you would notice changes.

New businesses were still opening. Grand Union opened at 103 Main Street with a special opening sale. Sugar was 10 pounds for 53 cents; flour was just 89 cents for a 24.5 pound sack; coffee sold for 19 cents a pound; pork loin roasts were 20 cents a pound; butter was 85 cents for two pounds and cheese sold for 29 cents a pound. Empire Chain Store Company opened at 107 Main to sell clothing. W. T. Grant's opened at 139 to 141 Main Street selling housewares, clothing and more. The Finger Lakes Association held a photo contest for photos to be used to promote the region in magazines, newspapers and booklets. The new Junior High building was being completed. When it opened in the fall, 1300 to 1500 attended the dedication. Still people were suffering. Residents were urged to shop locally.

In **1930** the Sampson Theatre closed. It was re opened and used as a miniature golf course complete with a little mountain with running water, gold fish and 18 holes which went up and down the aisles and on to the stage. This venture did not succeed. In 1938 the Sampson Theatre would become Jewett Motors sales and service department selling Dodge and Plymouth motor cars.

This image is from the 1930s. We are looking at the east side of Main Street. Lown's appears in the middle. If you look closely you can read the sign. To the left of Lown's is J. C. Penney's and then the Grant Company. (YCGHS)

Penn Yan Boats had received an order for 3,000 outboard boats from the Johnson Motor Company and needed additional factory space. They expected to produce 40 complete boats per day with two eight hour shifts and 300 men. This was fantastic news. 3500 attended the opening of the new boat factory. They did well for a while. Then the nationwide depression resulted in a decrease in demand and Penn Yan Boats was forced to cut production and release many of their employees. Michaels Stern also cut production closing down their Penn Yan factory that made coats. Farm prices went way down. The Chronicle Express promised to publish free situations wanted advertisements for the unemployed.

The population in Penn Yan in 1930 was 5,321. Gas drilling came to the area in 1930. Leases were filed with the County Clerk. They called for one well to be drilled on each property within a year of the lease being signed. If the well was not drilled in that time period the lease expired. If it was drilled, the lease could be renewed. Women were named to the board of the Yates County Agricultural Society for the first time.

On January 2nd, **1931** the Penn Yan Democrat published the following: "New Years day this year may seem to many folks a time for sad consideration of wishes more drably practical than hopefully gay. 'Happy New Year' if agricultural or commercial hard times are uppermost in ones mind may have a sound of hollow optimism. Yet pessimistic hard bargaining for better business cannot in itself work a miracle. We must go forward with a certain sureness of heart. This is the soundest kind of gaiety. It holds with wisdom that better times will develop from careful reasoning and good will."

Penn Yan's population was not sitting still. There was a relief committee that helped families in need of groceries, fuel and clothing. In the fall of 1931 the county considered a survey to see how many were unemployed. The towns decided this would be a waste of money. They could take care of their own. Come December a central welfare committee raised funds to provide for those in need for Christmas. It was made up of representatives from area schools and churches.

Things weren't all bad. More gas was discovered in Wayne, about 12 miles south of Penn Yan. There was a well just 200 feet from the church and another 50 feet from the corner store and garage. It would help meet expenses. Gas from Wayne was to be sent to Dundee for filtering and then to Horseheads and on to Binghamton. The Associated Gas & Electric Company and Lamoka Power Corporation requested franchises to pump gas to Hammondsport to serve homes, stores and factories. Lycoming Gas Corporation won a contract to pipe gas from the Wayne field to Penn Yan. This would bring some jobs to local residents.

Penn Yan Boat Company received an order for 700 to 800 boats which put some men back to work.

Prohibition did not end until 1933. Raids occurred on those who were making and selling illegal beverages. Speakeasies were raided in the village. A cottage on Bluff Point was found to have what appeared to be a complete manufacturing setup. They had 600 gallons of mash, eight 200 gallon vats, a bottle capper, four 50 gallon empty barrels, 50 feet of rubber hose, a 5 gallon copper container, three carbonated gas tanks, two wash boilers, 38 pounds of apricots, 11 copper funnels, a 50 gallon cooker and a 75 gallon container.

The early 30's found farmers suffering from the depression and from bad weather. A severe cold spell devastated the apple crop. Certainly people were hurting. There were frequent newspaper articles about men committing suicide. The American Legion encouraged people to stop holding back and start spending. Their message was "If you were planning on doing something before the depression do it now." Their theory was that holding back just made the situation worse; spending would result in someone getting a job.

In **1934** Walker Bin Company Inc. declared bankruptcy. They said that the expansion of chain stores who used different fixtures – rows of shelves and tables – and the depression which reduced demand for quality woodwork in churches and homes had resulted in the end of the company. The company was later revived as Walkerbilt. During WWII Walkerbilt made wooden products for war use. After the war it expanded making store fixtures, industrial wood parts, radio cabinets and custom wood work. In 1974 it was purchased by Haywood Wakefield Co. Five years later in 1979 it was bought by Pennsylvania House.

In 1934, thirteen million people were receiving relief from the Federal Government. There were four million in the Civil Works Administration, one million doing Public Works, and 297,000 in the Civilian Conservation Corps. Some people were concerned about how the Federal Government was managing the situation. They felt that the government was spending too much, increasing taxes and not thinking about how the budget would or could be balanced. They believed that the government was increasing control on private businesses through government bureaus and officials. Past history had shown that this would be destructive to the nation. They did not like the government's increasing involvement in establishing or subsidizing enterprises who were in competition with private businesses. They were concerned about increasing strikes and violent labor disturbances. They believed that people who presumed to speak for the government administration were destroying confidence in security of property and investments leading to people becoming increasingly nervous regarding the stability of the government and its financial integrity.

The National Chamber of Commerce proposed six questions to the Federal Government:

1. When and how will the Federal budget be balanced?

2. Is the Federal Government planning to further reduce the value of the dollar?

3. Will the Federal Government work with other nations to come up with a plan for the international stabilization of exchange?

4. Will the administration focus on encouraging businesses with a minimum of government interference and control and discontinue its activities in competition with private enterprise?

5. What is the administration's policy toward agriculture?

6. Is it the policy of the administration to continue construction and development of public works not now needed?

The average citizen was very concerned about the future. In **1936** the local paper, the Chronicle Express, promoted WPA jobs. New York Central Electric Corporation lowered their rates. Some people wanted diagonal parking on Main Street. They gathered together for a petition to make sure that was what happened. Others wanted parallel parking as they thought it would make more room for fire equipment. Penn Yan finally applied to WPA for money to widen Main Street. Meanwhile the WPA was rebuilding the road from Dresden to Watkins Glen. They were also taking up the trolley tracks in Penn Yan. It was the summer of 1936, the dust bowl year, that the area experienced an incredible heat wave with temperatures reaching 106 degrees in the shade. Lake levels fell significantly. Grape growers reported their yield for the year was going to be an average of 30% less than usual. The County Fair was promoting a double parachute leap, a balloon ascension, fire works, a big midway, home talent horse race, amateur night and a triple wedding.

1936 was also the year that the federal government announced Social Security taxes. They were to begin deducting taxes from workers' pay in 1937. If you had a weekly pay of $20 your tax would be 20 cents. When you turned 65 years old you would start receiving benefits. If you were age 20 now you would receive $11.71 per week when you were 65. If you were age 45 now you would be paid $6.88 per week when you reached age 65. The Market Basket grocery store advertised pork roasts for 17 cents per pound, 3 pounds of macaroni for 20 cents, a 22 ounce loaf of bread for 9 cents, Salada tea for 37 cents per half a pound, and Mah Jongg Coffee for 23 cents per pound. The new 1937 Hudson automobile 6 cylinder was advertised for $695.

In **1937** the Elmwood movie theatre was showing Mickey Mouse to kids providing admission and candy for just ten cents at the 1:00 p.m. show. Washington passed a bill requiring a 25 cent per hour minimum wage and a maximum work week of forty four hours.

In June the "Behind the Scenes of American Business" column in the Penn Yan Democrat reported industrial production was down to the level it had been in 1932. Still there was optimism that it would recover soon. Factory employment was up in ten industries: farm implements, iron and steel wire, cash registers, engines and turbines, machine tools, aircraft, women's clothing,

Elmwood Theater located on Elm Street just west of Main Street. The theater was a popular attraction in Penn Yan. It was a conversion of the old Shearman House, a hotel which was built in 1839. (YCGHS)

baking, beverages and rayon. WPA money came to Penn Yan to help pay for the new Junior and Senior high school, a grade school, garage and a heating plant. The buildings were expected to cost a million dollars. The money Penn Yan received was $607,500. With the consolidation of the school district Penn Yan would have 2400 students.

In August there was a terrible flood. Rain poured down for 12 straight hours and equaled four and a half inches. It was the worst flood the village had ever experienced. Water was neck deep in the Penn Yan Creamery; 18 feet flooded the Birkett Mills boiler room; Barden & Robeson Basket factory had 3 feet of water in the mill; and on Champlin Avenue 7 homes had water up to the second floor. Still the paper reported that manufacturing was reviving. By the end of the month the report was that the outlook for businesses was excellent. In October, steel and auto workers were busy again, as was paper manufacturing. In November, retail furniture sales went up. Ford Motor Company said they planned to expand in 1939 and were spending thirty four million dollars on new plants. The recovery had started and stock prices were going up. Life was getting better.

There is much more to Penn Yan's story. To learn more about it, pick up the book *Penn Yan & How It Got That Way* or visit the Yates County Genealogical & Historical Society.

Now that you know some of the highlights of Penn Yan's early history, take a walk along Main Street, with the tour book in hand and take a close look at the buildings. You will find pictures of some of the buildings as they once appeared along with a timeline to help you discover what was happening when each building was constructed, and details about each structure. Our walk along Penn Yan's Main Street begins at the Arcade building, 144-150 Main Street. The first section of the tour covers the Commercial District. We will walk south along the west side of Main Street and return along the east side. The Residential District will follow. This time we will walk north up the west side of Main Street and return along the east side. We hope you enjoy the tour.

Historic Images of Penn Yan's Main Street

Main Street in 1868. This is a post card image of Penn Yan's Main Street as it looked in 1868 looking south toward the Mill. The road is still dirt. Many of the buildings had roofs covering the side walk. Carriages were parked on an angle. (YCGHS)

Main Street in 1868. In this postcard we are looking at the west side of Main Street, south from the corner of Elm Street. You can see Armstrong & Gage's Hardware store at the right edge of the picture. This would become Pinckney Hardware in 1945. (YCGHS)

Main Street looking North from Jacob Street, Penn Yan, N. Y.

Looking north on Main Street from Elm Street in the **1890s**. Toward the middle of the picture you can see the Cornwell Opera House and the buildings north. (YCGHS)

This **1890s** image is from just south of the Knapp House which you can see on the left side. Note the power poles along Main Street. (YCGHS)

This **1907** image shows the east side on Main Street north of East Elm Street. (TPC)

Looking south from the east side of the street near Maiden Lane in the **1920s** you can see the Citizens Bank in the right foreground and a sign for the Metropolitan painted on the brick side of the building. In the distance on the right you can just make out the tower on the Hollowell & Wise Hardware store (now Pinckney's Hardware). (YCGHS)

Looking north on Main Street in the **1920s** you can see the tower on the left side which was a part of the hardware store which would become Pinckney's Hardware. Towards the right middle of the image you can see the steeple of the old Presbyterian Church on the corner of Clinton and Main Streets. This image is a photograph by Burnell. (YCGHS)

Here is an image from the **1920s** of the east side of Main Street looking south from the west side near Maiden Lane. You can see the little firehouse, the second building from the left, on the west side. (YCGHS)

This picture was taken in the **1940s** from the Benham House. You can see the portico at the front. (TPC)

In this image from the **1940s** you can see Pinckney Hardware in the middle with the tower. (TPC)

In this image from the **1940s** you can see Pinckney Hardware on the left side and the drug store in the middle. (TPC)

In this picture from the late **1940s** you can see the old Keuka Restaurant in the right foreground and the Chronicle building on the left side. (TPC)

IMPORTANT EVENTS IN HISTORY
1763 – 1939

1763	Proclamation of 1763 prohibits settlement west of line
1764	Sugar Act; Currency Act
1765	Stamp Act followed by violent reaction
1766	Stamp Act repealed
1773	Tea Act followed by Boston Tea Party
1774	Intolerable Acts; port of Boston closed
1775	First battles of the Revolution, near Boston
1776	Declaration of Independence
1778	French American Alliance
1779	Sullivan-Clinton Campaign
1781	General Charles Cornwallis surrenders to General George Washington at Yorktown; Articles of Confederation signed, nation is born
1783	Treaty of Paris
1786	***Treaty of Hartford, settles NY State boundaries***
1788	***Phelps-Gorham Purchase;*** Haudenosaunee sign treaty; ***Universal Friends settle near Dresden***
1789	Constitution goes into effect; George Washington becomes President; ***Ontario County organized***
1790	***Universal Friends settlement has a population of approximately 300; Ontario County Organized***; Constitution ratified
1791	Robert Morris buys land; Bill of Rights ratified; ***George Wheeler buys lot 37; David Wagener comes to area; first settlers come to Penn Yan***
1792	***Pulteney Estate buys land***; Washington re-elected President; ***Lot 37 split***
1793	Cotton Gin invented making slavery profitable again
1794	Treaty of Canandaigua; Whiskey Rebellion; ***Birdsall builds sawmill at Outlet in Penn Yan***
1795	***Dr. John Dorman comes to Penn Yan***
1797	John Adams becomes President
1799	George Washington dies; ***David Wagener dies; Main Street surveyed***
1800	Population of the US = 5,308,483; ***on New Year's Day Abraham Wagener moves into first frame house in Penn Yan; Penn Yan has 9 households***
1801	Thomas Jefferson elected President; ***Abr. Wagener becomes postmaster, builds 2nd grist mill in Penn Yan, has road built from Canandaigua to Newtown***
1802	***Wagener Bridge built over Outlet at Mill***
1803	Louisiana Purchase; Meriwether Lewis & William Clark explore west

1807	Fulton invents steamboat
1808	US Slave trade with Africa ends; ***Abr. Wagener becomes Justice of Peace***
1809	James Madison becomes President
1810	***Penn Yan has about 20 households***
1812	War of 1812; James Madison re-elected President
1813	***Abr. Wagener builds Mansion House***
1814	Francis Scott Key writes the Star Spangled Banner
1815	***John L. Lewis teaches school in village; Penn Yan has 40 houses and 300 residents;*** War of 1812 ends
1817	James Monroe becomes President; ***Wm & Dr. Andrew Oliver move to Penn Yan***
1818	***Abraham Bennett starts 1st newspaper in village – Penn Yan Herald;*** Congress adopts present design of US Flag
1821	James Monroe's second term as President begins
1823	***Yates County organized with Penn Yan as county seat; population = 11,000;*** Monroe Doctrine proclaimed
1824	***First Church in Penn Yan – First Presbyterian Church; 2nd newspaper est. Yates Republican***
1825	Erie Canal completed; John Quincy Adams President
1826	***Religious revival in Penn Yan; Barrington, Starkey and Dundee join Yates County***
1829	Andrew Jackson becomes President
1830	Second Great Awakening religious revival movement begins
1831	***William M. Oliver founds Yates County Bank; Geo. Shearman builds American Hotel***
1833	***Crooked Lake Canal complete; Penn Yan incorporates; Abraham Wagener becomes 1st mayor;*** Andrew Jackson begins 2nd term
1834	***Abraham Wagener moves out to home on the Bluff***
1835	***Penn Yan establishes 1st Fire Company; 2nd Court House built by Enoch Bordwell; First steamboat, the "Keuka", provides service on Keuka Lake***
1836	***Brimstone Row fire; grape industry begins***
1837	Panic of 1837
1839	***Penn Yan organizes brass band***
1840	***Yates County Agricultural Society organized***
1841	William Harrison becomes President and dies in office; John Tyler becomes President
1845	James Polk becomes President
1846	Wilmot Proviso; US – Mexican War begins
1849	Zachary Taylor becomes President
1850	***Canandaigua & Elmira Rail Road comes to Penn Yan;*** Zachary Taylor dies; Millard Fillmore becomes President; Compromise of 1850
1851	***Methodist Wesleyan Meetinghouse built at 300 Main Street***

1853	Franklin Pierce becomes President
1854	**Abraham Wagener dies**
1855	**Penn Yan population = 3,000; Women's Rights Convention in Penn Yan**
1857	**Penn Yan Union School District incorporated**; James Buchanan becomes President; Dred Scott v. Sanford; Panic of 1857
1859	John Brown's raid
1860	South Carolina secedes; **Benham House built; Penn Yan Gas Light Co. organized**
1861	Abraham Lincoln becomes President; Civil War begins at Fort Sumter; Jefferson Davis elected President of the Confederacy; **Keuka Rifles go to war.**
1862	Emancipation Proclamation issued, takes effect in 1863
1864	**Charles V. Bush builds Bush's Hall which later becomes Cornwell Opera House**
1865	Civil War ends; Lincoln assassinated; Andrew Johnson becomes President; 13th Amendment passes
1869	1st Transcontinental Rail Road completed; **Struble's Arcade built by Charles V. Bush @ 144 – 150 Main; Knapp Hotel built**
1870	**First winery in area erected**
1871	**First Baptist Church at 224 Main built, 2nd on site**
1872	**Great Fire of 1872 in Penn Yan**
1873	Panic of 1873
1874	NYS passes compulsory school law; **Women's Christian Temperance Union chapter formed in Penn Yan**
1875	**Tourist Industry begins in Yates County**
1876	Alexander Graham Bell invents the telephone
1877	**Crooked Lake Canal abandoned; mill owner syndicate purchases right of way for Penn Yan and New York Railway Company**
1879	Thomas Edison invents the light bulb
1880	US population exceeds 50 million
1881	James Garfield becomes President and is assassinated; Chester A. Arthur becomes President; Clara Barton creates Red Cross
1885	Grover Cleveland becomes President
1887	**Penn Yan and New York Railway incorporated**
1889	Benjamin Harrison becomes President; **C. V. Bush builds Lown's**
1890	**Keuka College founded; Ball Hall built**
1893	Grover Cleveland becomes President; Panic of 1893
1897	**Trolley service begins**; William McKinley becomes President
1898	Spanish American War begins; **Methodist Church at 168 Main built**
1900	
1901	McKinley assassinated; Theodore Roosevelt becomes President
1902	**Penn Yan telephone service begins**; Olds Motor Vehicle Co. sells cars

1903	Wright Brothers make first flight
1905	***Steam powered electric plant built in Penn Yan; Library built with Carneige grant***
1906	***Penn Yan's population almost reaches 5,000; first street paved w/brick***
1908	***Curtiss has 1st witnessed flight; Soldiers & Sailors monument constructed in Penn Yan***; Ford Model T appears on the market
1909	***Yates County goes dry***; William Howard Taft becomes President
1911	***Susannah Hatmaker opens Hospital in Penn Yan***
1913	Woodrow Wilson becomes President; 16th Amendment establishes income tax
1914	World War 1 begins in Europe
1917	US enters World War 1
1919	Treaty of Versailles ends WW 1; 18th Amendment establishes Prohibition; ***Penn Yan's Home Defense Committee decides to build hospital as a memorial to soldiers and sailors***
1920	19th Amendment gives Women right to vote
1921	Warren G. Harding becomes President
1922	***Steamboat service ends on Keuka Lake***
1923	Harding dies; Calvin Coolidge becomes President
1924	***Soldiers & Sailors Memorial Hospital opens***
1925	
1927	Charles Lindbergh makes first trans-Atlantic flight
1928	***Trolley service between Penn Yan and Branchport ends***
1929	Herbert Hoover becomes president: crash of 1929; ***Penn Yan's new Junior High School opens***
1930	Birdseye creates frozen vegetables; ***Penn Yan population = 5,321; Sampson theater closes; Penn Yan Boats and Michaels Stern cut production; gas drilling comes to area***
1933	Franklin Delano Roosevelt becomes President and establishes New Deal; 21st Amendment ends Prohibition
1934	Glass Steagall Act; US Securities and Exchange Commission established: Johnson Act; Reciprocal Trade Agreements Act; Tydings McDuffie Act; Share the Wealth Society founded; ***Walker Bin Co. goes bankrupt***
1935	FBI Established; Neutrality Act; Social Security Act; Revenue Act
1936	Second London Naval Treaty
1937	Neutrality Acts; Hindenburg disaster
1938	Wheeler Lea Act; Fair Labor Standards Act
1939	Hatch Act; Nazi Germany invades Poland and WWII begins; President Roosevelt becomes the first President to give a speech broadcast on TV

This map shows what Penn Yan looked like in 1854. An original map hangs in the Yates County Clerks office. (GRL)

A WALK ALONG PENN YAN'S MAIN STREET

A WALKING TOUR MAP

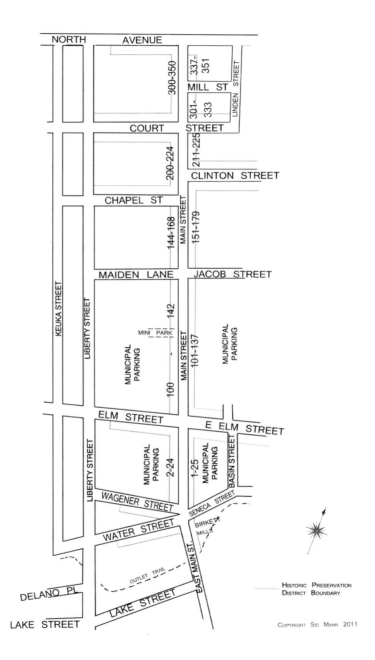

COPYRIGHT SID MANN 2011

HISTORIC PRESERVATION
DISTRICT BOUNDARY

THE WALKING TOUR

As we begin our walk it is important to keep in mind that the village was not settled from the Post Office out. As you learned in the early history of Penn Yan, the first buildings to appear were at the north end of Main Street at the four corners of Main and what was then called Head Street. Next came the mills at the south end of Main Street along the Outlet. As with most old villages the dates of the current buildings jump around. A time line is located on page 64 to help you keep track of what was happening when each building was constructed. For more detailed information on Penn Yan, in chronological order, pick up a copy of Frances Dumas's book *Penn Yan & How It Got that Way.* Fran is the Yates County Historian as well as the local public historian for both Penn Yan and Milo.

We begin our tour in front of Struble's Arcade, 144-150 Main Street. When Penn Yan was first settled in 1791 the business section was located at Head Street (now North Avenue) and there were some log cabins situated along Jacob's Brook. Businesses did not begin moving to the current business district till the 1820s.

Penn Yan's Historic Commercial District

This is an image of the Arcade from the 1876 Yates County Atlas. You can see the wrought iron on the top of the roof.

Our first building in the Commercial District is on the west side of the street heading south. It is **144-150 Main Street.** This is **Struble's Arcade**. All this land was owned by Abraham Wagener. About 1814 he sold 100-122 to G.D. and Samuel Stewart and 124 to 150 to William Howe of Benton. Howe sold it to Dr. Dorman's wife Sybil. After Dr. Dorman died in 1821 it was inherited by his granddaughters Betsey Nichols and Susan Miller. They sold it to Samuel Ellsworth. He sold it to Alexander Cole. It was

144-150 Main Street. The old Arcade building with the portico in the front. Notice the wrought iron railing on top of the portico. (YCGHS)

then owned by Alfred Brown, followed by Alfred Brown and G.R. Youngs. When Charles V. Bush purchased this lot from Brown in 1867, the Post Office was located in a small wooden building on the southeast side. There were also two houses. Bush built the Arcade in 1869. A prominent architect and builder, he moved to Penn Yan in 1848. Here he built most of the commercial buildings on the east side of Main Street as well as on the west side, from 144 to 118 except for 126. He introduced the first plate glass store front in Penn Yan and built both the Yates County jail and Penn Yan Academy.

The Arcade with its shops and offices was the forerunner of today's indoor shopping malls and was rare in old commercial districts. It is one of a very few still in existence. In 1876 it was purchased by Charles D. Welles. Clinton B. Struble, an attorney and prominent businessman, purchased the Arcade in 1898. He was surrogate clerk, and served as president of the village and a member of the board of trustees. Struble owned a great deal of real estate in the area. In fact he owned Esperanza, a mansion overlooking Keuka Lake's west branch, in the 1920s. He sold it to the County for a County Home in 1926.

The Arcade is one of the most significant buildings in the village. The original front of the building had a series of arched windows on

144-150 Main (GRL)

the first floor. There was a cast iron balcony which extended along the second floor on the facade. It is General Grant/Second Empire style. The brick was made locally, as was most of the brick used to build the stores in Penn Yan, and was painted for protection. The stone veneer you see covering the brick at the front on the first floor today was added in modern times.

For a while the first floor housed an A&P market, said to have been one of the first in the chain. The village's first telephone exchange was located here in 1902. It moved to a new central office at 138 Elm Street with a new switchboard in 1929. At that time there were 2000 telephones in Penn Yan, an average of one for every three people. The post office was located in the back before it moved across the street in 1912. When it was decided that the post office would move, Struble seriously considered moving the telephone offices to the front of the building and making an opera house in the back. That was never to occur. The second floor had 18 offices and businesses, including attorneys, insurance offices, a photographer, a watch maker, a dentist and the draft board for World War I and II. The third floor was used by the GAR (the Grand Army of the Republic – a fraternal organization of Union Army veterans) and the American Legion as a hall. At one point stairs led down from the sidewalk to the basement level. The level of Main

This image clearly shows 138 Main – Shutt's Grocery, 140 Main Street - Citizens Bank, along with 142 Main and the Arcade building, 144 – 150 Main Street. (YCGHS)

Street has changed since then. The lower level housed a barber shop, a meat market, a bakery, two restaurants and at one time even contained an Oyster Bar.

In 1935 the Village Directory listed the following businesses located in the Arcade: A & P Tea Company, the Penn Yan Democrat, the Town Clerk, David Miller - Insurance, Needle Craft, the Public Welfare Office, Harry P. Morgan - barber, H. R. Sanford - news dealer, J. F. Osborne – correspondent for the Elmira Star Gazette, the Rochester Times Union and the Rochester Democrat Chronicle, the Penn Yan Credit Bureau, Abram Gridley - lawyer, National Re-employment, Mutual Realty Company, Penny Ann Advertising Company, Lake Keuka Vineyards and Lynch Robertson Shoppe – a dry goods store. To enter the Arcade you went in through a central door which led to a main corridor with doors opening into various businesses and a stairway leading to the top floors. Many businesses have called the Arcade home over the years.

We are now crossing **Maiden Lane**. There once was a school located on Maiden Lane where there is now a parking lot. The Maiden Lane School was built in 1842. It was a large barn like structure with three rooms and three teachers. Like other schools of that time it was heated with a wood burning stove. There was a belfry on the roof and it had two entrances – one for girls and one for boys. The school was abandoned in 1893 when the Liberty Street school was erected. Owen Hoban converted the building into a hitching stable. In 1931 Edward G. Hopkins constructed the Maiden Lane Parking Station. It was a gas station with room for parking cars. A farmers market was held there on Wednesdays and Saturdays. One Saturday 1,000 people visited. It was torn down to make way for the parking lot we see today.

142 Main St. (GRL)

In 1850 there was a vacant lot from Maiden Lane till you reached the Metropolitan at 126 Main Street. It was surrounded by a six foot high fence. There was a lot of excitement in Penn Yan when a hot air balloon ascended from approximately where 142 is located today.

The building we see at the corner is **142 Main Street**, the home of the Keuka Lake Association. In 1838 Dr. Dorman's granddaughters' guardians, Alfred Brown and George R. Youngs, sold the vacant lots where buildings numbered 142 through 132 are located. In 1848 this whole area was a vacant lot. The property where 142 is located was sold to E.L. Jacobus. Some time before 1890 there was a two story stepped gable building located here. The brick building's window sills and lintels were made out of wood. At that time many buildings had false fronts above their top floor windows. This building may be that two story building as it was not uncommon for commercial buildings to be updated to an Italianate look. In 1913 the first floor was occupied by Harry O. Bennett, a druggist. In 1922, Sharp & Co., a millinery store was here. In 1927 it was Ruth William's millinery. In 1938 this was Deckerman Brothers, a book and stationery store.

140 Main in 2012
(GRL)

140 and 138 Main lots were sold to Nathan Kidder and Henry Bennett in 1850 by Brown and Youngs. They built buildings which they rented out to other businesses.

The **140 Main** that we see today was built in 1873. It was the site of the First

Another image of 140 Main, from the 1876 Yates County Atlas. It depicts the First National Bank which was the first bank on the site.

140 Main c. 1914 (Wolcott)

National Bank. In 1911, Citizens Bank, chartered in 1899, remodeled the building making architectural changes. It was at that time that the stone Classic Revival facade was added. The top section of the arch

138 Main St. (GRL)

was filled by a three panel window. Citizens Bank was still at this location in 1938.

138 Main Street was built about 1875. The third floor windows have stone lintels and sills. The first floor has been set back about two

This image shows 138 Main Street when it was L. P. Wagener's Grocery. You can see their delivery wagon in front of the store. Next door is 136 Main Street which was Wagener Brothers Shoe Store at the time, the early 1900s. (YCGHS)

feet. In 1900 this was the location of L. P. Wagener's Grocery. In 1913 it was Shutt's Grocery. Burnell Studio, a photo and art store, occupied the building in 1927. It was still there in 1938. The building was

| 132 Main | 134 Main | 136 Main (GRL) |

later used by Home Savings & Loan of Penn Yan which was purchased by Columbia Banking. From 1968 until 1971 it was Tilton's Bookstore.

136 Main Street. This vacant property was sold by Brown and Youngs to William Briggs in 1852. Later that year Charles V. Bush built this building. It has stone sills and lintels on the second floor windows with an intricate Italianate cornice. In 1900 it was occupied by the Wagener Brothers Boots and Shoes. Their shoe factory was first located behind the Central House, now the location of the Once Again Shop on East Elm Street. In 1913 it was the home of Bush's Music Store. Then in 1927 Thomas Bagley's Restaurant was located here. In 1938 it was the location of Reilly Brothers, a music and electric appliance store.

This picture is of 132 Main Street, Bush's Music and Electric Appliance Store, c. 1960. (YCGHS)

The property where 132 and 134 are located was sold by Brown and Youngs with 134 going to James Burns and Howard Miller in 1853 and 132 to Abner Bridgman in 1855. It is likely that there were buildings on both sites in the 1830s.

Buildings **132 and 134** were also erected in the 1850s by Charles V. Bush. The front facade of 132 was altered in 1925 by Warner Bush. 134 had a fifteen foot extension made to the west about 1925. The large plate glass windows and tile work at the front occurred about 1935. In 1900, 134 was H. C. Guthrie, Bookseller, Stationery etc. The Crystal Florist occupied the site in the early 1920s. In 1935 it was the location of George Pappas, florist. Number 132 was the location of H. Merton Smith's Shoe Store in 1900. It was also home to the Gem Photo Company. In 1913 it was Elbert Wells Fargo Express Office. A well known local jeweler, Fred Roese occupied the store in 1920 – 1922. In 1925 it became Bush's Music and Radio House and remained that into the mid 1970s.

130 Main Street (GRL)

130 Main Street was built in 1861 by George McAllister as an Italianate style building. The first building on the site was built by Anson Wyman in 1838. The first occupant of the current building was David Gray and Company, a menswear store. In 1900 it was home to N. K. Sherman's Department Store. In 1913 it became the New York Shop and Penn Yan Light and Gas Company. It was later occupied by the New York Central Gas Corporation. In 1935 it was the home of New York Central Electric Company. Then it became a New York State Electric and Gas office. Offices were located on the second floor. The facade was altered in 1942.

128 Main Street doesn't exist. 126 Main, now Henderson Drug, is wider than most store fronts and was assigned 126, skipping 128.

126 Main Street, where Henderson Drug is located today, was built about 1840 by Anson Wyman as a meat market. At that time it had a step-gabled roof and the brick facade was painted gray. Myron Hamlin bought the property in 1857 for his emporium called the

126 Main, the Metropolitan before it received it's new 1889 facade. (YCGHS)

126 Main, the Metropolitan, after the facade was changed in 1889. (YCGHS)

Metropolitan. His son, Theodore Hamlin, ran it until 1937. Advertisements for the Metropolitan in 1920 showed the following products for sale: dresses, suits, coats, skirts, gloves, bathing suits, underwear, fabrics, trims, oil cloth, patterns, aprons, towels, rugs, electric sweepers, straw suitcases, and even wallpaper. In 1889 the building was enlarged and the facade changed to the dark red brick and brownstone we see now. This is Richardsonian Romanesque style. You can see Hamlin's name and the date the store was founded near the top of the building.

In 1909 the Masonic Hall was on the third floor. The Metropolitan closed in 1937 and Loblaw Groceteria moved in. Henderson's Drugs has been here since the mid 1960s. The first and second floors are rock faced Medina stone. Notice the leaf motif carvings between the arches on the second floor windows.

The property where 126 and 130 are located was sold to businessman Samuel Stuart Ellsworth by Dr. John Dorman. Ellsworth was quite the business man. He helped build the various stage lines to and from Penn Yan and was involved in the building and running of the steamboat *Keuka*, the first steamboat on Keuka Lake. He was also connected with the produce trade and transportation on the Canal. He and Spencer Booth established a mercantile, produce, lumber and farm supply business in Branchport. Ellsworth was the supervisor of Milo, county judge and a member of the Assembly. In 1844 he was elected to Congress. While there he suggested that new states be admitted to the Union under the same conditions that Thomas Jefferson set up in the Northwest Ordinance of 1784. It prohibited slavery in new states and territories. Representative Wilmot of Pennsylvania enthusiastically promoted this idea and the Wilmot Proviso came to be. It was one of the major events that led to the Civil War. The proviso would have banned slavery in any territory acquired as a result of the Mexican War along with lands in south Texas and New Mexico east of the Rio Grande. Ellsworth sold 126, and 130 to Wyman.

126 Main Street today (SM)

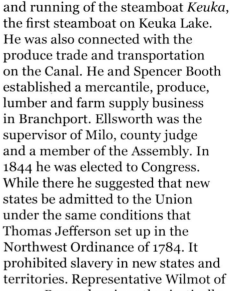

124 Main was sold to G.D. Stewart by Dr. Dorman in 1819. The building here was built about 1830 as a three story Greek Revival building – notice the eyebrow windows. In 1900 Dr. C. Elmendorf had his medical practice here. In 1909 it was a millinery shop. In 1922 a popular lunch restaurant occupied the building. From 1925 until 1970 it was Roese's Jewelry store. Then it became a Singer Sewing Machine Shop, which was followed by an antique store. Unfortunately when the building was remodeled they took away much of its beauty.

124 Main Street (GRL)

80

Urban renewal resulted in the little park we have here today where **120 and 122** would be located. The Stewart Brothers bought the lot that included 100 through 122 Main Street in 1813 from Abraham Wagener. The brothers sold this property to Samuel S. Ellsworth, who sold it again, but kept the lots for 100 and 102 at the corner of Main Street and Elm. There he built a large general store, which remained at that location for many years. 120 through 122 were built in the 1840s and had wooden facades. 120 was built by Henry Bradley in 1848. One was often a coffee shop or a restaurant. In 1935 number 122 was Excell Boot & Shoe Company. George Excell took over the McAdams Shoe Company in 1916 turning it into his own store. He

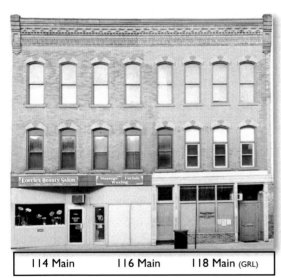

114 Main   116 Main   118 Main (GRL)

was a member of the Odd Fellows, the Masons, the Grange and the Penn Yan Fire Department. He operated the Excell Tourist Camp on Lake Street until 1954. Number 120 was then Rapalee Drug Company.

Number **118** was built by Henry Bradley in 1848. It was the home of A. M. Bernston's Tailor Shop and Arthur Jessup's harness shop in 1900. Richard Craugh's bakery was located here in 1913. In 1922, it was the New York Shop, a ladies clothing store. In 1927 it became the Cash Food Store. In 1935 it was the home of the Market Basket.

116 Main was the location of Citizens Bank and Sisson's Insurance in 1900. In 1913 it was McAdam and Kinyoun's Clothing Store, with a dentist on the second floor. In 1922 it was Mary Dervan's Millinery Shop.

The facade of **114** was changed about 1875. It is a brick building with an Italianate cornice. Notice the monograms in the windows' keystone arches. In 1900 it was occupied by E. H. Hopkins, Jeweler and Optician and Wheeler Brothers Grocers. Hopkins was replaced by Jared Darrow, Jeweler and Optometrist and George Eillis, an optometrist. Then came George Jewelers and Watchmaker's business. In 1938 it was Robert C. Schmidt's Jewelry store. From 1970 to 1976

| 108 Main | 110 Main | 112 Main (GRL) |

it was Miller's Music Store. Then it became the Deacon's Bench.

The old store fronts had recessed doors and plate glass windows. Before plate glass was available the windows were still glass, but with small panes. The store fronts also had large awnings with signs indicating their name.

112, 110 and 108 Main Street. This section of buildings were built in 1875 and modified in the 1930s and 1960s. The windows on the upper floors have stone sills and lintels. The buildings are topped with ornate brick cornices and once featured one of the best Art Deco style facades in the village. This Art Deco facade was on the ground floor and is now covered up. **112** was the Boston Shoe

112 Main Street was Brownbilt Shoes in 1938. Here you see the exterior of the store in the top picture and the interior in the bottom. (YCGHS)

82

Store in 1900. In 1927 it was the Wagener Brothers Shoe store with John L. Hastings, optometrist on the second floor. In 1938 it was M. C. Stark Clothing Company and Brownbilt Shoe Store. **Number 110** was F. W. Steelman's grocery in 1900. In 1913 it was C. M. Conklin & Brothers Clothing, along with Thomas Carmody, attorney and Frank McAdams, tailor. In 1927 it was the Endicott Johnson Shoe store, along with the Yates County Farm & Home Bureau. Endicott Johnson Shoes was still there in 1938. **Number 108** was the Smith Shoe Store in 1903. In 1913 Hans P. Hansen, a tailor was upstairs and H. Merton Smith Shoes remained downstairs. In 1927 the shoe store remained along with a tailor, a chiropractor and a girls business club.

The stores located here were originally built of wood and part of Brimstone Row which burned in 1836. Afterwards the village building code required that buildings be made of brick. This section is all one building with fire walls in between.

104-106 Main St. (GRL)

As you can see, the current store at **104 and 106 Main** Street has a wooden facade. In the past there were often three occupants of these two buildings with two businesses in 106. The middle door led to the second floor where there were offices. The third floor sometimes held residences. In 1938, Shepard & Grady jewelery store occupied the main floor and C. Eugene Shepard, optometrist, the second floor. 106 was Mallory and Grantier, clothiers.

In 1968 the corner of Main and Elm Streets, **100 and 102 Main**, now the Riedman Building, was a victim of urban renewal. George Sherman owned the original building. T. F. Wheeler Druggist & Apothecary was located here in 1894. He sold "pure drugs", chemicals, paint, oils, varnishes, wall paper, toilet and fancy goods. In 1904 he became partners with Ernest Bordwell. The building was next occupied by Bordwell's Drugs Inc. Ernest R. Bordwell came to Penn Yan from Pennsylvania in 1857 and went into the drug store business with his father. For a long time this building was a drug store with doctors' offices above.

Bordwell Drugs carried a full line of paints, oils, varnishes, cigars and such as well as prescriptions. The store had a curved corner and was quite attractive. As you can see from the picture of the store, it had the same curved front that Pinckney Hardware across the street has today. Bordwell's was still located at 100 in 1938. Number 102 was Quay's Delicatessen in 1935. In 1936 it was Hanscom's Ice Cream Bar and Restaurant. Quay's had moved to 120 Main.

Here is 100 Main Street when it was Wheeler Drug Store. Typical of the old store fronts the business name appears on the awnings. (YCGHS)

Bordwell's Drugs was once located at the corner of Main and Elm Street. Ernest Bordwell was first a partner with T. F. Wheeler in Wheeler Drugs. When he took over the store the name was changed. Bordwell's eventually moved to the Lake Street Plaza. Be sure to notice the curved corner of the store. (YCGHS)

100 Main Street today (SM)

At an earlier time there was a grocery store at 102. It was called the "Pine Tree Grocery" and was owned by Amasa Tuell. The store's name was due to a large pine tree that stood next to the sidewalk near the bank of the Outlet. Yes, the Outlet's bank used to be here. It is said that the meeting to come up with a name for the village was held under that pine tree in 1805. The tree was used as sort of a bulletin board for the village. The story goes that a group of residents gathered at the tree to discuss a name for the village. After much argument with both those who had come from Pennsylvania and those from New England wanting a name that reflected their heritage, an agreement was finally reached and the name "Penn Yang" was chosen. It was later shortened to Penn Yan. The current village Indian arrow head shaped emblem depicts two men, a Pennsylvanian and a Yankee, shaking hands. The grocery store was destroyed in the fire of 1836 taking the tree with it.

The Outlet was moved in the late 1820s when they started building the Canal. The Outlet and the Canal were separate with the Canal located on the north side. The mills which were here at the time were raised a whole story. Everything from Elm Street south was on the bank of the ravine of the Outlet which was so steep that stairs were required to reach it. At that point East Elm Street was called Jacob Street. For a while number 100-102 was a mini park. The village decided to sell the property and the new modern building you see here today was put up.

Before you cross the street look west on Elm Street. Where the Village Hall is located today was once the Shearman House, a hotel erected in 1839. In 1920 it was purchased by Harry Morse, the

This 1907 postcard shows the Shearman House and a trolley. The Shearman House was a hotel which was located near the corner of Elm Street and Main. The hotel was converted into the Elmwood Theater. (YCGHS)

steamboat captain who as a boy caught a trout with his nose, for a theatre. His plan was to tear down the building and replace it with a theatre with two stores in front. The entrance would be through a lobby and vestibule. It would seat 600 with the possibility of adding additional balcony seating for 112. It was to be called the Elmwood Theatre. As it turned out they modified the old hotel. The entrance to the theater went through the front. When the theater opened in 1921 there were 650 seats on the first floor and 150 in the balcony. Tickets sold for $2.50 each. When the theater closed the building became the home of the Penn Yan Racquet Club. It was razed to build the new, current,Village Hall in November 2003.

Crossing over Elm Street we come to **24 Main Street.** The building that stands here now was built in 1985. It replaced the original building which was built about 1834. That building was owned by Abraham Wagener. He sold it to Daniel Bissell and Willliam Oliver. In 1841 the site was owned by Whitney & Stark; then Whitney, Ayres & Stark. They were followed by Watson, Stark & Company and Alfred Rose's "Cheap Store." In 1853 it was L. E. Lapham's grocery. In 1861 Armstrong & Gage Hardware store was located here. They expanded into a building just west of them on Elm Street in 1864. In 1885 it was Hollowell & Wise, hardware. Wise was William N. Wise the "grape king". He acquired that name because he

Hollowell & Wise Hardware was located at 24 Main Street when Edward Pinckney Sr. purchased the store which became Pinckney Hardware. This c. 1900 postcard illustrates what the building once looked like. (YCGHS)

Taken about 1912, this image shows the inside of Hollowell & Wise Hardware. (YCGHS)

Pinckney Hardware before the fire of 1985. At this time 20 and 22 Main had been included in the store. (YCGHS)

shipped so many grapes. Hollowell & Wise owned the property when Edward Pinckney Sr. purchased the building in 1945. When it was Hollowell and Wise the first floor was the main part of the store. On the second floor they had home furnishings. The top two floors were used for plumbing and storage.

The fourth floor was added in 1881, the glass was changed and some windows added on the second and third floors facing Main Street. There was once a hipped roof with a conical tower which was removed in 1952.

A fire broke out in Pinckney's Hardware in March 1985 at 4:30 in the morning when a gas heater over heated and ignited the ceiling. It was a significant fire and effected 20, 22 and 24. All these buildings were torn town. As you can see in the picture, the previous building was made of cream colored brick with a curved front just like the store on the opposite side of the street. Pinckney Hardware rebuilt after the fire, keeping the curved corner of the original architectural style.

Number **22 Main** was connected to 24 in 1966 and the facade modernized. It once had a stepped gable roof with a balustrade across the top. Number 22 was McLeod Tobacco Shop with a cigar factory

Pinckney Hardware as it appears today. (GRL)

This is an image of 22 Main Street when it was McLeod Tobacco House in the late 1800's. (YCGHS)

on the third floor in 1889. In 1914 they became the Penn Yan Tobacco Company. They remained there until Pinckney Hardware expanded in 1966.

Numbers **14 – 20 Main** Street were originally built in Greek Revival style during the 1830s and 40s. They were updated with Italianate features and additional floors were added. The heavy upper cornice was removed after 1922, and the store fronts were modernized in 1967. This was the block where Abraham Wagener originally built his farmhouse called the "Mansion House". His mother's house had been located here. He moved her house when he built his new home and planted his orchard. In 1876 number 20 was George Lapham's grocery store. In 1889 it was McMath and Morgan grocers. They later moved to number 12 Main and were replaced by Kelly and Corcoran Grocers. In 1938 this was the location of the Commodore Restaurant.

18 Main Street (GRL)

Number 18 was Quenan Brothers Grocery in 1935. In 1938 it was the Great Atlantic & Pacific Tea Company (A&P).

16 Main Street (GRL)

Number 16 was built in 1838. By 1857 it was a grocery store owned by John Lapham. In 1938 it was the location of Rushmore's Eldora bakery and the Elite Beauty Shoppe. It was originally a two story Greek Revival commercial structure modernized into Italianate. It has a very elaborate detailed cornice and cast iron columns at the front. The upper section above the belt was added about 1875.

Number 14. About 1865 it was a paint store owned by George Wells. After that it was Edward Wilkinson's drug store. Then in 1879 it was Frank Quackenbush's Drug Store. After Quackenbush moved it was Variety Stores Inc. By the early 1930s it was the John J. McGovern paint store.

14 Main Street (GRL)

Number 10 – 12, the current Keuka Restaurant facade is new – perhaps since around 2000. There has been a restaurant at this location for a long time. The building was built in Second Empire

12 Main Street, McMath & Morgan Grocery (YCGHS)

Main 10-12 The Keuka Restaurant c. 1960 (YCGHS)

10-12 Main, The Keuka Restaurant today (GRL)

style, unusual for small towns, the same style as the Arcade. At one time there was iron grillwork along the roof. The palladian roof dormers give it a distinctive look. The windows on the second floor are Italianate. The facade on the street level was modernized in the late 1930s into an Art Deco style. It is covered now with a new facade. This building was built with two store fronts. William H. Watson was likely the original builder. He was a brewer and bought the property in 1840. At one point he owned the Pinckney Building, number 24 Main. In 1899 Keuka Steam Laundry occupied number 10 and McMath & Morgan Groceries were in number 12. A little later Robeson's Groceries was in number 10. They remained there until 1932 when a Shoe Repair store occupied the building. In 1935 the Keuka Restaurant took over number 12 and soon expanded into number 10. The current Keuka Restaurant opened in 2007. The new owners kept the name of the old restaurant.

2 Main Street. Knapp Hotel c. 1905. Note the wrought iron on top of the mansard tower (YCGHS)

2 Main Street, The **Knapp Hotel** was built in 1876-1877 by Oliver C. Knapp. He was the manager of the Crooked Lake Navigation Company for a while. This land was part of Abraham Wagener's farm.

Here you see what the Knapp House Hotel once looked like. Notice the wrought iron on the top of the portico which opened out on to Main Street. You can also see the Keuka Restaurant property next door as you look up Main Street. c. 1900. (YCGHS)

2 Main Street. Knapp Hotel today (GRL)

His house, the Mansion House, was later used as an inn. When the Knapp Hotel was built the Mansion House was moved to where the Sampson Theater is today. The Knapp Hotel was more graceful then than it appears today. It is Italianate in style. Notice the mansard tower. Built three stories high in brick it had 37 rooms. In 1916 the village considered purchasing the building for the village offices, the fire companies, the police court, the jail, the clerk's offices and board rooms for both Penn Yan and Milo. It would have been expensive to renovate and the public voted it down.

An elaborate two story porch was removed from the Main Street side where the building was recessed in 1937.

In 1945 the hotel was modernized with an addition where the porch was once located. The iron columns along the Main Street side were manufactured by Cheney Company of Rochester. The original marble fire places on the upper most floor are said to still exist. There was a dining room on the first floor that could accommodate 100 guests. Also on the first floor were a ladies' parlor, a large office and a writing room. It had an elegant front. When you look at the picture, notice the portico that once extended out into Main Street. The door was on the side. There were shops on the first floor with doors opening out onto Main Street, just as there are today. In 1935 the shops were as follows: number 8 was Western Union Telegraph Company, number 6 was Welch & Messinger – barbers, and number 4 was Postal Tel Cable Company.

In 1916 the Knapp Hotel was owned by Charles H. Mitchell and his son Arthur from New York City who made some updates. They also owned the Benham Hotel.

Number 1 - 5 East Main Street is known as the Chronicle building. It was built in 1889 to house the Chronicle Express' offices and print shop. The Chronicle Express began as the Yates Republican. The first issue was on December 16th, 1824.

1-5 East Main Street (GRL)

At that time it was located on Head Street. In 1831 the Yates County Inquirer was the paper. It was discontinued after two years. In 1837 the Democratic Whig came to be owned and operated by William Child. In 1839 the name was changed to Yates County Whig by Nicholas Suydam. Then in 1852 Stafford C. Cleveland took over and the paper became the Yates County Republican. Next, in 1876, it became the Yates County Chronicle. In 1873 another newspaper was started by Reuben Schofield – the Penn Yan Express. In 1926 the Penn Yan Express and the Yates County Chronicle merged and became the paper we read today, the Chronicle Express.

Early in Penn Yan's history there was a saw mill located here. When the Chronicle building was built in 1889, this was a vacant lot except for a dock which was used by the Knapp House hotel. The Chronicle building was built over the guard lock of the Canal. As late as 1920 the measurement of the lake's level was made from the sill of the building. Notice the Romanesque rustication (an architectural term for a feature that is rough and contrasts to smoothly finished surfaces) of stonework, brick and terra-cotta features on the exterior. You can see the building's date high above the entrance.

In 1900 the first floor housed L. P. Wagener's Grocery, Penn Yan Gas and Light Company, and the Penn Yan Water Works. During the period of 1913 through 1922 Shutt's Grocery was on the first floor. In 1927 Burnell Studios was located there. In 1971 the Chronicle Express moved their offices to 138 Main Street and their printing to Hammondsport. The building was later purchased by Columbia Banking. Finally in 1971 the upper floors were converted into apartments.

Under the sidewalks are large steam tunnels. Steam generated by Birkett Mills was supplied to the Penn Yan Steam Heating Company. It heated most of the businesses on Main and Elm Streets, as well as many residences, with a mile of steam lines. In 1948 Birkett Mills stopped generating steam and alternative methods of heating were needed.

The Wagener bridge was built at the mill in 1802. It was replaced with one that crossed over both the Outlet and the new Canal. In 1857 the Main Street bridge was about fifteen feet lower than it is today. The bank was so steep that people had to go down a flight of stairs to reach the bridge from the businesses at the end of Main Street. In 1884 the bridge was raised a story and the mills were moved back 17 feet. When the canal closed, the State auctioned off all the bridges and the locks. Much of the stone in the current Main Street bridge is canal

Penn Yan in 1873, View looking South.

This image looking south is of the Main Street bridge about 1873. The sign at the start of the bridge reads, "15 [CENTS?] FINE TO DRIVE ACROSS THIS BRIDGE FASTER THAN A WALK" (YCGHS)

stone, some of the same stone that was used in the replacement of the original wood locks.

In the 1860s and 1870s businessmen found the Canal inadequate for their needs. They wanted fast, inexpensive transportation for their goods. The Canal never made a profit and in 1877 it was officially abandoned. Mill owners formed a syndicate to purchase the right of way with the intent of building a railroad between Penn Yan and Dresden. The railroad they built was called the Penn Yan and New York Railway Company. Those men were William Fox, Oliver Shearman, Seneca Pratt, Calvin Russel, Perley Curtis and John Andrews. In 1883 they owned part of Seneca Mills, Milo Mills, Shutts' Mill, Fox's Mill and the two gristmills at the dam in Penn Yan. A new bridge was built at Main Street to cross the Outlet to make room for the railroad. The railroad ran along the south and east bank of the Outlet. In Penn Yan the railroad went under Main Street and split with one branch going under Liberty Street and out to the lake and the other crossing where the other trestle is, terminating on Water Street at the malthouse where the "castle", currently the property of NYSEG, is today. A passenger station was located behind the malthouse that Oliver Shearman built on Canal Street. An ice house was built at the lake and large warehouses were built along the waterfront. Shipping fresh fruit was now possible.

There were two railroads coming into the village. The Canandaigua Elmira Railway became the Northern Central and then the Pennsylvania. The Fall Brook Railway or the Penn Yan and New York Railway Company, along the canal, became part of the New York Central.

Birkett Mills, c. 1900 (YCGHS)

Birkett Mills from the Main Street bridge, c.1915. (YCGHS)

Birkett Mills, c. 1960-70's (YCGHS)

Our next building of interest is **Birkett Mills**, located at the corner of Main and Seneca Streets. Study the building for a moment before you cross over the street. Note that East Main Street is an extension of Main Street, starting at Water and Seneca Streets going south across the bridge. Main Street goes north from this point.

Birkett Mills was originally built in 1801 as a grist mill; it burned in 1824 and was immediately rebuilt. The lower two stories replaced the original mill. It was the second grist mill in Penn Yan. While you are looking at the building be sure to notice the Greek Revival vernacular door. In 1846 the wood machinery was replaced with that made of iron. A syndicate purchased the mill in 1882. They made some improvements

Greek Revival vernacular door (GRL)

Birkett Mills today (SM)

including adding two more stories. They retained the gambrel roof and moved the structure 17 feet to the east onto its present foundation. Calvin Russel and Clarence Birkett took over the mill around 1890. The mill was expanded in 1900, 1910, and 1913. The brick addition toward the back of the building and the silos were added in 1924. The griddle mounted on the side of the building was used in 1987 to make the world's largest buckwheat pancake – 28 feet one inch in diameter. Birkett Mills is the largest producer of buckwheat products in the world. The mill is usually in operation five days a week, 16 hours a day. But in the early fall, during their busy season, the mill operates 24 hours a day. You can purchase their products at the mill's office, 163 Main, or at many grocery stores.

Seneca Street was called Canal Street in 1833. Many warehouses were located along Canal and Water streets during the days of the canal. The only one left today is located at 131-133 Water Street.

According to the 1854 Penn Yan map, there was once a canal boatman's hotel called the **Owls Nest** located down Seneca Street to the east. On the map it was shown as a dotted line because it was destroyed in a fire which originated there. The fire also destroyed some of the buildings on Main Street. "Owls" were the ladies that hung out of the upstairs windows. It seemed that until the mid 1850s the police were often arresting these "ladies". The old Owls Nest was rebuilt on Water Street as a cold storage building for fruit which was shipped on the Canal. When they rebuilt there were saloons located at numbers 1, 3 and 5 Main Street.

I Main Street (GRL)

Number 1 Main has a paneled brick entablature similar to that of number 14 Main. A cast iron store front and a pressed tin ceiling can be found on the first floor. Note the monogramed windows. You can see the same motif on 101 Main Street. 1 Main was built about 1880 by Charles V. Bush and replaced a building which had burned.

Number 3. The building once here and the ones on either side were all destroyed by fire and rebuilt. This building was built by D. H. Ackley as a saloon. He also used it as a hotel. Julia Baron was the next to own number 3. She lived upstairs. A hotel for several years, it

3 Main Street today (GRL)

was also in succession a saloon, a pool parlor, a Chevrolet dealer, a restaurant, a barber shop and now is Lloyds Limited, a popular pub. When the 18th amendment made the sale of alcohol illegal, a speakeasy was located in the basement. You could enter through the back door of number 1 Main Street. When prohibition was repealed in 1933, the R and M Grill, which was located here at that time, was the first bar in Yates County to serve a legal drink.

In 1935, number 1 was Circle Supply – an auto supply and accessory store, number 3 was Nelson's Sandwich Shop, and number 5 was Charles F. Stratton's restaurant. Buildings that were built about 1880, or who had their facades remodeled, had that special look. Number 1 had a story added.

The R & M Restaurant was once located at 3 Main Street. In 1933 it was the first restaurant in the village to serve an alcoholic beverage after prohibition was lifted. (YCGHS)

Number 5 has a beautiful cornice. Also note the lintels over the second floor windows. The store front was modernized in 1965 and again in 1977-78. Stratton's restaurant's booths were built by Walkerbilt and can still be found inside.

| 9 Main | 7 Main | 5 Main (GRL) |

Numbers 7 – 9 Main were built about 1880 by Charles V. Bush. There was a building on this site in 1834 which was destroyed by the Owls Nest fire. This whole block had stores in 1834. This building was a hotel and a saloon till about 1912. Then it became a commercial building. In 1927 and 1938 W. M. Corcoran & Son hardware store was located at number 7, and Martin F. Craugh, billiards, was at number 9. He was still there in 1935. In 1938 it was the location of Fred C. Murphy's restaurant.

The building we see today at **11 Main** Street was built about 1880. It has been occupied by various businesses such as Shannon Farm Implements in 1889. In 1900 it was a saloon. It became a tobacco and hardware store in 1913. McGreevy Sales Corporation sold tires and batteries here in 1920. In 1927 it was George W. Peck Hardware Company. Eckert's Grocery and Meat Store was located here in 1933. In 1938 it was once again G. W. Peck Hardware. A hand pulled elevator was still operational in 1985.

11 Main Street (GRL)

13-17 Main Street (GRL)

Numbers **13 through 17 Main** were built in 1875. You will notice that the attractive cornice is very similar to several others in the business district. It was once the Sheridan House Hotel. Then it became part of McGreevy Sales which was located next door at number 11. In 1927 I. E. Eckert's Store (a grocery store), Habberfield and Company (a meat store) and Frank Quackenbush's Drug Store were all here. In 1935, Habberfield Grocery was still at number 13 and number 17 was Penn Yan Baking Company. In 1938 grocer Larsen & Clark Inc. was located at 13 Main.

Number 19-23, the current Milly's Pantry and the Cafe Next Door, is the Odd Fellows Building. The Odd Fellows, or Three Link Fraternity, believe that friendship, love and truth are the basic guidelines that one should follow in life. By working with their communities members make a difference in the lives of the people who live there. The organization began in 18th century England and came to the United States and Canada in 1819. It's very appropriate that Milly's Pantry is located here today. In 2011 Milly Bloomquist received a Presidential Citizens Medal at the White House from President Obama. It was Milly who created and continues to operate many of Penn Yan's programs designed to help those in need, including Food for the Needy, Christmas for the Needy, and the Weekend Backpack Program for Yates County. This building is the second oldest in this block. The oldest is number 25 Main Street.

In 1897, when the trolley went to Keuka Park, the building only went up to the

19-23 Main Street (GRL)

first cornice. This building has had very little alteration otherwise. It was built about 1835. Eben Smith and his son Franklin E. Smith owned it. Eben had previously been in the hardware business. His son was a clerk at his store. This store was a clothing store – E. & F. M. Smith & Company. Franklin Smith was part of the group of business men who organized the Penn Yan & New York Railroad along the Outlet.

25 Main Street, c. 1865 (YCGHS)

In 1891 the IOOF bought the building. They added the fourth floor and the elaborate top. The first floor was rented to various businesses – a hardware store, a tailor, a barber, a businessmen's association, and a candy store. The top floors were used for meetings and banquets. The top floor has a large meeting room with a beautiful tin ceiling and a raised platform running around three sides which was used for ceremonies. Today this space is used for several activities including dance and yoga classes. On the floor below, the Odd Fellows had a kitchen, a dining room and some additional space. In 1920 the membership of the Odd Fellows totaled 450. In 1909 there was a liquor and tobacco store at number 17 and a confectionery at number 19. In 1938 numbers 19 through 21 were the location of The Market Basket, a small chain store out of Geneva. Number 23 was Seward's Candy Store.

Built about 1825, **number 25** has a stepped gable Federal Style facade and an elliptical vent opening on the north side. If you look at the south side of building number 101, across East Elm Street, you will notice that they both have these features. The store that was located here burned in 1840, but not completely. The top story was added about 1890. You can see some of the alterations which have been made by looking at the changes in the brick. This was once the site of Nelson Tunnicliff's dry goods store. In 1885 it was a liquor and tobacco store. In 1912 it was The Senate Restaurant. Then in 1927 is was occupied by a pharmacy and a tailor. In 1935 it was Prouty & Waldron drugs.

25 Main Street today(GRL)

The first buildings located at **numbers 101 and 103** were built in 1836 by Eben Smith. He sold 101 to James Dwight Morgan to be a hardware store, called Morgan's Hardware. It was the

101 Main St. today (GRL)

103 Main Street, c. mid 1950's (TPC)

village's first hardware store. It originally had a Federal style front and stepped gables. Charles Morgan followed his father in the hardware business. Next it was a men's clothing store. There was a hall on the third floor. The Central House,

103 Main St after altering, c1990 (GRL)

a hotel, was located next door on Jacob Street (now East Elm Street), in the building that now houses the Once Again Shop.

Charles V. Bush built the current building at 101 in 1885 with three

103 during alteration, April 2012 temporarily showing the old sign "CHILDREN'S TOGGERY" (GRL)

floors. 101 was Seely Clothing Company and the Moose Hall in 1922. Wallace, Platman & Boyd were located there in 1938 along with optometrist Lewis A Gracy and dentist J. H. Wheeler. In 1889 T. S. Burns had a grocery store at 103. There was a door to the second floor of both buildings. In 1900 it was Durnin Saloon. It was the Public Market in 1922. In 1935 it was used by a dentist and an optometrist and was the location of the Grand Union grocery store. In 1938 it was Brown & Hopkins grocers. Longs' Cards & Books was located here before they moved to the Cornwell Opera House building. It is a good example of Italianate Commercial style. The first floor facade of 101 was altered in the 1990s and 103 was altered in 2012. Look at the sides of 101 and 25, the Pizzeria, and you can see how the street level has been raised. This occurred in 1897 when the trolley line was built.

Before you move on, stand at the corner of **East Elm and Main Streets** for a few minutes. Look east and imagine what it was like when the whole area east of this building was destroyed by the Great Fire of 1872 that was mentioned in the early history of Penn Yan. On April 30, 1872 about 4 o'clock the call of "FIRE" was heard. People ran from their businesses to see where it was. The fire started on the roof of the Commercial Iron Works which was located on East Elm Street where the Masonic Temple building stands today. Firemen rushed to the scene, but with little water and a strong south wind they were unable to put the fire out. The planing mill of Cornell & Waddel, in the back, caught fire and was destroyed along with all of the

About 1912, looking down Jacob Street from Main street (now East Elm Street). It clearly shows 101 Main on the left and 25 Main on the right. (YCGHS)

In 1909 looking down East Elm Street. This image shows the Central House which was located where the Once Again Shop is today. The Sampson Theater was yet to be built. East Elm, or Jacob Street as it was first called, was once a very busy area. (YCGHS)

lumber. The fire spread quickly and consumed over 50 buildings and about 50 acres. The Canandaigua Fire Department sent their steam engine on a special train. They arrived in time to stop the fire from spreading further. Still the losses were substantial. Fortunately all the buildings on Main Street from here to the Benham House were saved. The Benham House was located where the Community Bank is today.

105 through 109 Main are all one building which was built in 1858. The American Hotel fire of 1857 burned all the way to 103 Main. This building was built by J. T. Rugg. The wooden cornices and the copper framed plate glass window supports on the first floor are unusual. 105 was F. W. Horton's Opera House Bakery in 1889. It became the Olympian Fruit and Candy Company, 1900 through 1927. In 1938 it was P. G. Costes's Restaurant. Notice the iron grillwork covering the eyebrow or frieze windows. In 1889, 107 and 109 were together as Eaton Brothers Groceries. It was a book store for several years. Curran Florist and Cigars were in number 109 in 1889. New York Telephone, along with several lawyers and insurance offices occupied the space as well. In 1935 number 105 was a coffee shop and a beauty shop. Number 107 was Tilton's Book Shop along with the Penn Yan Dry Cleaners and the Alcoholic Beverage Control Board. 109 was Hyatt's Karmelkorn Shop and a beauty shop. This building is one of the few original Greek Revival structures that did not have alterations above the second floor level.

111 – 119 Main Street are one building, built in 1864. **111** is at the south end of the Cornwell Opera House building. Patrick Hendrick owned the lot in 1860. Various businesses have called this home over the years. In 1850 it was Tracy

105-109 Main Street today (GRL)

& Miller Croton's store. The Penn Yan Express newspaper was here from 1889 to 1922. Donaldson & Hess Company, a clothing store, was here from 1912 to 1927 along with lawyer, Mr. Fiero, from 1912 to 1922. In 1935 J. J. Newberry Company occupied numbers 111 through 117. There were others located there as well: a dentist, Coopers Public Market, the Sample Dress Shop, and Knapp's Beauty Shop. Geneva Travel Agency moved here in March 1977. Today it is Frames Galore & More.

113-119 Main Street   111 Main Street (GRL)

Numbers 113 through 119. Longs' Cards & Books which uses 115 for their address, is on the original site of the American Hotel. The hotel was built in 1831 by George Shearman. At the time it was the best hotel in town. Supervisors held their meetings there. Stage coaches stopped there; many bachelor merchants lived there and it is said to have been the social center of the village. In September 1857, while local firemen were having an excursion to Hammondsport, a fire destroyed the hotel and five businesses south to 103, leaving a vacant lot.

Charles V. Bush built Bush's Hall in 1864. It opened for functions on December 20th of that year. On the first floor were three businesses; the Post Office occupied the store at the south, John M. Latier Dry Goods was in the center, and Cornwell's Book Store was at the north. The entrance to the hall was from the south up some stairs. On the left side where you now see some metal panels, there was a passageway to the lot behind the building where there was once a livery stable. Bush sold the building to Harvey Easton in 1866. Easton then sold it to George R. Cornwell in October 1872. In 1858 Cornwell had a bookstore on Main Street at a different location. He moved his store to the first floor of Bush's Hall. In addition to books, stationary and wall paper, he sold sewing machines and musical instruments. When he purchased the building he converted the upstairs hall into Cornwell's Opera House. A stage was constructed at the east end of the hall. Many speakers, plays and events were held both at Bush's Hall and the Cornwell Opera House. Susan B. Anthony, a prominent civil rights leader, Frederick Douglass, leader of the abolition movement, Ralph Waldo Emerson, and Phineas T. Barnum are just a few of those who spoke there.

In 1903 this was the location of the YMCA. Nathaniel Sackett opened a movie theatre in the hall in 1910 where silent movies were shown. It was also used as the Grange Hall and as the Christian Science Church. Inside the recessed panel at the top of the building it used to say "Cornwell's Opera House", as can be seen in the picture on the next page. The steel circles are turnbuckles which hold the building together.

In 1892 the upstairs was converted into offices because there were so many halls and theaters competing the hall was not needed. Then in 1907 a fire destroyed the Lyceum Theatre, which was located at 129 Main Street, down a right-of-way to the north. A long hallway led back to the building from the Main Street entrance. Cornwell's Opera House was used for shows again. In 1988, the building was a Rite Aid Pharmacy. It was being renovated when a fire broke out in the new office. Fortunately it was contained but the firemen had to break through the corrugated fiberglass covered upstairs windows to let the smoke out. Longs' book store purchased the building in 1990 and restored the windows on the second floor. Longs' Cards & Books first store was located at 107 Main Street in 1969. In 1981 they moved to the corner of Main and East Elm, number 101 Main.

This is an 1874 picture of the Cornwell Opera House. You can see the George R. Cornwell book store on the left side of the picture. Just to the left of it was a passage way to the livery stable located at the rear of the building. There were often three stores on the first floor. The post office was once located where Andrew MacKay Grocers appears, on the far right. The entrance to the opera house was up a flight of stairs to the right of the store. (YCGHS)

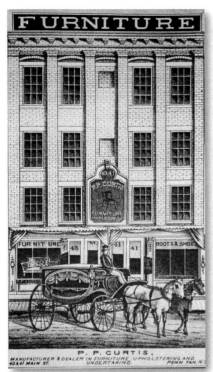

This image from the 1876 Yates County Atlas shows 121 & 123 Main Street when it was the Curtiss furniture store and shoe store.

121 and 123 Main Street

were one building built about 1841, with two store fronts, by Eli Sheldon. He had his business, a dry goods store, on the first floor and a public meeting room on the second floor. The building had a double store front. In 1867, after Curtiss' furniture factory on the corner of Main and Clinton burned, Samuel and Perley bought this building, altered the facade and added another story. They had their furniture store with undertaking in the basement in the northern store front and a shoe store in the southern. In 1869 Samuel Curtiss sold his interest in the shoe store to J. Henry Smith. In 1870 he sold his interest in the furniture store to John T. Andrews. Perley retained his interest in both stores. The shoe store was then Curtiss and Smith, while the furniture store became Curtiss and Andrews.

In 1881 the businesses were bought by B. Borgman and Son. The furniture and undertaking business became Knapp (Clarence H.) and Borgman in 1888. It was common for furniture stores to also make caskets. In 1896 Charles B. Curtiss sold the block to George R. Cornwell, owner of the Cornwell Opera House next door. Charles V. Bush replaced the facade with a late Victorian style in 1901 and the Corcoran Brothers moved their furniture business to this location. In 1911 they purchased the building. They were still located there in 1935. The old hand pulled freight elevator is still in use today. Stop for a moment and notice the various different materials used on the facade of this building.

121 and 123 Main Street today (GRL)

111

INTERIOR VIEW OF
W.W.QUACKENBUSH'S
DRUG STORE.

DEALER IN
DRUGS, PATENT MEDICINES,
FANCY AND TOILET ARTICLES,
PAINTING MATERIALS &C
No.28 MAIN ST.
PENN YAN, NEW YORK.

Quackenbush's Drug Store was once located at 125 Main Street. This is an image from the 1876 Yates County Atlas which shows the inside of the store at that time.

Number **125 Main**, the current Nest Egg Gift Shop, dates back to the mid 1830s. This lot was the end of Dr. Dorman's 4 acre homestead lot which went from 159 Main to 127 Main. The first store here was built by Alfred Brown. Thomas Hendrick purchased the property in 1852 and built a meat market

in 1864 — Hyland & Caviston meat market. In 1867 W. W. Quackenbush opened his pharmacy here. He carried drugs, toilet articles, paints, oils, varnishes and other sundry. Messrs. Dewan and Huson & Hyland, lawyers were also located here through 1927. In 1935 it was the home of F. Quackenbush Drugs. In 1944 it was sold to Lourance Prouty who sold it to Adelaide Holliday for "The Holliday Shop". The first floor of the

125 Main Street (GRL)

building has obviously been altered. It is said that the counter now used by the Nest Egg gift shop was once part of a soda fountain.

Number 127, the Maxwell Building, was built in 1872 as Baldwins Bank by Charles V. Bush. The lot was vacant at that time. It was a brick building with stone arches outlining the first story bays. The vault inside had a 17 ton door. The second floor was occupied by the law office of Morris Brown and Ralph Wood. In 1936 a major renovation was done to the interior. Security Trust bought the

127 Main Street during the 2012 alterations (GRL)

BANKING HOUSE of M. L. BALDWIN,
SILAS KINNE, CASHIER,
PENN YAN, N.Y.

127 Main Street was once the location of Baldwin's Bank. This image from the 1876 Atlas shows how the building once looked.

building from Baldwins Bank in 1958. They changed the look considerably. It has since been modified again. At one time it had a semicircular cornice decoration like that at number 130. It was raised to three stories and then reduced back to two stories. You can still see where the third floor windows used to be. There was a right of way between this building and the next one giving access to number **129 Main**, the Yates Lyceum & Opera House. First named Sheppard's Opera House in honor of Morris F. Sheppard, it was built in 1890. It had a capacity of 800 and was said to be one of the finest village theaters in the country. In 1905 Cecil B. Demille played the title role in *Lord Chumley* there.

In 1907 a fire broke out in the store room under the balcony, while the minstrel show "The Hottest Coon in Dixie" was going on. 330,000 gallons of water were poured on the blaze. Unfortunately the watchman at the time died in the fire. Many near by buildings were also destroyed, but none on Main Street.

The Sanborn map on the next page shows the location of the opera house.

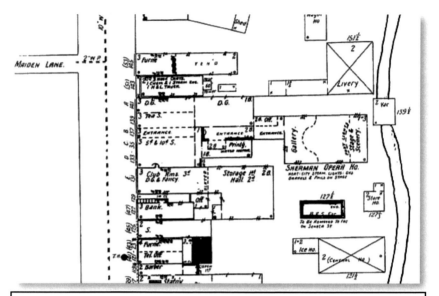

1903 Sanborn map showing the location of the Yates Lyceum & Opera house. The opera house labeled as the Sherman Opera House in error on this Sanborn map was first Sheppard's Opera House. It was named the the Yates Lyceum & Opera House when it burned.

131 Main Street today (GRL)

Number **131 Main** was the site of the Yates County Bank from 1833 to 1857. The private banks of Stark and Rapalee were located here through the 1870s. In 1871 Lown's, then Jones & Lown, was located where T. F. Wheeler's Drug Store used to be at the corner of Main and Elm Streets. In 1877 Jones and Lown changed their business name to J. H. Lown and Company. In 1889 Charles V. Bush constructed the current building for J. H. Lown's Dry Goods business. Lown's sold dry goods, carpets, millinery, crockery and glassware. The new store added several departments – fancy glassware, lamps, bric-a-brac. The carpet department was enlarged and said to be better than anything found in western New York outside of Rochester. Lown's was known for its female clerks. In the 1880s most clerks were male. George Lown took over from his father. In 1903 Lown's

Lown's window display in the 1930s. (YCGHS)

Inside of Lown's. (YCGHS)

merged with Cassius N. McFarren who managed the store from 1903 till 1912. Next Issac L. Yetter became president of the company. In 1946 James Curbeau and Son from Elmira took over. The building has been a department store until recently. Initially the upper floors of the building were used as commercial space, storage for stock and as apartments. The Odd Fellows, Keuka Lodge used the third floor meeting hall from 1899 to 1922.

Notice all the different materials and styles used in this building. There is a Moorish influence. The battlemented cornice terra-cotta and brick detailing are significant. The first story capitals and pilaster story and lintel corner blocks add to the building's beauty. The different and unusual windows on the second and third floors should also be noted. Inside you will still find the apparatus used when it was a department store to transfer payments, sales slips and change from the sales clerks to the cashier. This Lamson Cash Carrier System was invented in the late 19th century as a business tool. It was in service here for almost 100 years. The Smithsonian visited the store to take a video of the Lamson Cash system in operation. These systems were very popular in retail stores throughout the country. Very few exist today.

131-141 Main Street, c. 1975 (YCGHS)

Next door you will find the current Elks Lodge, **133 Main** and Milo's Town Offices, **137 Main Street**. This used to be a 90 foot wide department store, Roenke & Rogers, which extended into the land that is now used for Jacob Street. It was **number 133 through 141**. Built by Charles V. Bush, it replaced Eben Smith's

137-141 Main Street today (SM)

116

house in 1888-1889. In 1909 it was a five and ten cents store. J.C. Penney occupied the building in 1929. They were still there in 1935. W. T. Grants occupied the building to the north, numbers 139 – 141. It burned when the little fire station located at 143 caught fire in 1967 and was later taken down by the village. The buildings located here today were put up in the early 1970s.

In 1856 there was a small firehouse located at **143 Main Street** between the A&P number 145 and Lown's. It burned in 1884 and was rebuilt. In 1916 it was renovated. The station was just big enough for two engines. A ramp led down to the road over the curb from the fire

This picture shows what the little fire station located at 143 Main once looked like. You can see Eben Smith's house next door. (YCH)

station, Engine House #1. On December 20th, 1967 about 8:00 a.m. the building caught fire. Firemen were just arriving for work. They stood helplessly and watched as the doors burned and a fire engine rolled out and into the street. Fortunately people were able to prevent the burning engine from reaching the stores on the other side of the street. The second fire engine was towed out of the building. The firemen had no water or equipment so fire companies came from Dundee, Bellona, Keuka Park, Dresden, Branchport, Wayne and Geneva to put out the fire. The fire burned out of control for three hours. The A&P next door was destroyed. The Thompson Furniture

Firemen trying to save the A&P grocery from the flames at the Fire House in 1967. (YCGHS).

This picture from the newspaper shows the burned pumper truck which was destroyed in the fire. (YCGHS)

Store which was located on the other side suffered smoke and water damage. Ironically two nights before the Village Board had voted to go out for bids to build a new fire station. American LaFrance loaned the village two fire trucks. While the new fire station was being built on Elm Street they used the Penn Yan Express trucking company facilities on West Lake Road as a temporary fire station.

151 Main Street today, the Community Bank (GRL)

Where Community Bank is now located, number **151 Main**, was the Benham House. DeWitt Clinton Benham built the hotel on a mostly vacant lot about 1858; it remained there until 1960. The hotel was partially a residential hotel with stables and stage coach barns at the back. Amasa Tuell owned the stage coach line. It was a beautiful building, four stories high with a cupola on the top. It had a marvelous dining room. This area was part of the residential district until 1860. Adams Express Company, like today's parcel

The Benham Hotel, built in 1860, was popular for its dining room. (YCGHS)

Another image of the Benham, c. 1910. (YCGHS)

shipping companies, was located in the hotel. This lot was all part of the four acre lot Dr. Dorman bought from David Wagener in 1799.

Dr. Dorman had Thomas Clark, the same architect and builder who later built Jemima Wilkinson's final home in Jerusalem, build him a house here in 1800. It was the second frame house in the village and was built into the side of the bank. It looked like an

119

The post office as it looked when it was first built, c. 1912. (YCGHS)

The post office as it looks today. The only significant change is the steps and ramp going up to the front door (SM).

A-frame from the street. The Dormans lived on the lower floor. For years it was called the "Old Red House" because it was painted a bright Spanish red color. When the Benham Hotel was built the red house was moved and used as Charles V. Bush's shop. It was later moved again further up the street and destroyed in 1867.

We are now at the **Post Office, the Federal Building**. It was built in 1912 in a Georgian Revival style and placed on the National Register of Historic Places in 1989. The village's first post office was in Abraham Wagener's frame house on Main Street in 1800. In 1818 it was said to have been in the Penn Yan Herald newspaper's print shop on Head Street (now North Avenue). In 1833 it is supposed to have been in a small building on the southwest corner of the lot next door to the Baptist Church. In 1842 it was in the American Hotel. From 1864 to 1869 it was in the Cornwell Opera House building. In 1869 it was at the site of the Arcade building. It was also located in a building which was later occupied by Sears & Roebuck in 1888. In 1893 it moved back to the Arcade building where it remained until the current building was completed.

The first house on this lot was built by Nelson Thompson, the manager of the American Hotel. In 1863 there were two houses here. The second one was cut in two and moved to Champlin Avenue. Oliver Bryant purchased Thompson's house in 1863. In 1871 it belonged to Ira Rapalee. The lot was finally sold to the U.S. Government in 1909 and the house was moved to Elm Street.

This concludes our tour of the Historic Commercial District. This might be a good place for you to take a break. The second part of the tour covers the Historic Residential District. The tour of the residential district will begin across the street from the post office at 158 Main Street. You will walk north up the west side of the street to North Avenue and return along the east side of the street to this location.

Penn Yan's Historic Residential District

We continue our walk along Main Street, this time studying Penn Yan's Historic Residential District. We begin this part of our tour standing on the west side of Main Street opposite the Post Office at the Fox Inn Bed & Breakfast. Until 1824 Main Street was the only residential street in Penn Yan. The street was bottomless mud when wet and a dust bowl when dry until it was paved in the 1920s. Trees were planted along the street at the same time.

Please stay on the sidewalks and do not trespass. Remember, all the homes on this tour are private property.

158 Main Street (GRL)

158 Main Street. When this house was built, around 1820, it stood alone. If you looked south down Main Street you would have seen mainly scrub pine, a few bushes and perhaps a pine tree or two. The dirt trail was just wide enough for a wagon. The mills were located at the end of the trail on the Outlet. This house was originally built of a buff yellow brick with red penciling on the bricks. There have been very few additions made to this structure. The porticos on the sides and the back were added. It is an early example of a Greek Revival mansion with a temple front and Ionic columns supporting a

1876 Yates County Atlas drawing of William's house and his law office.

grand entablature. The columns are tree trunks covered with pieces of wood. It was built by William Morrison Oliver. The lot stretched all the way to what was to become Liberty Street.

William and his twin brother, Andrew moved to Penn Yan in 1817. William purchased this lot from Abraham Wagener because he wanted to hold elected office. At that time a man needed to be a property owner to hold office. William became Yates County's first judge of the Court of Common Pleas, holding that office from 1823 to 1828 and again from 1838 to 1845. He was lieutenant governor in 1830.

In 1831 William founded the Yates County Bank and was its President until it failed as a result of the panic of 1857. The bank was first housed in his small two room law office next door. You can see it on the right side of the image from the 1876 atlas above. His law office was a small replica of this house. The bank was moved to a new building at 131 Main Street about 1833.

Oliver was elected to Congress, a position he held from 1841 to 1843. In 1844 he was clerk of the Supreme Court of New York. When the Yates County Bank went bankrupt in the panic of 1857, he used his own money to pay back all the depositors. In 1865 he retired to a farm in Torrey.

William's twin brother was Dr. Andrew Ferguson Oliver. The brothers were the only sons of Andrew Oliver, a Presbyterian

Reformed Church traveling minister. Young Andrew studied medicine and was licensed as a physician and surgeon in 1813 by the Otsego County Medical Society. He became the founder of Yates Medical Society and served as its president many times. Andrew was also a delegate to the State's Medical Society and a mason, a Master of Penn Yan's Vernon Lodge and high priest of the local chapter of the Royal Arch Masons. He and his first wife had three children, Peter Oliver, Dr. William Oliver, and Jane who married John L. Lewis, Penn Yan's first school master. Dr. Andrew's son Peter married Maria Anna Clark Brown, the widow of James Brown Jr., Jemima Wilkinson's steward for many years. Peter acquired his uncle William's house and with Maria raised Brown's daughters there.

In 1858 this property was owned by George R. Youngs. In 1898 the house was bought by William H. Fox who owned a large paper mill on the Outlet. Fox started his first paper mill in Pittston, Pennsylvania in 1860. He moved to Penn Yan, and with his brother started Fox's Mill on the Outlet in 1865. The mill was originally built in 1823 as a saw and grist mill. The Fox brothers converted it to a paper mill. They made brown wrapping paper out of straw pulp. By 1870 the mill employed 9 men and 2 women. Perley P. Curtiss, son of Samuel F. Curtiss, the furniture maker, joined the business

This picture shows Edson Potter's house, 160 Main Street, with the Yates Lumber Company truck in front. The lumber company was expanded to make baskets. You will remember the Climax baskets which appeared on page 28. (YCGHS)

in 1882. In 1935 their paper mill was the oldest in the country still making straw paper and the only one east of Ohio. Their paper was sold throughout the United States, and in Cuba and Mexico. When wrapping paper was no longer in demand they switched production to crinkled and corrugated cartons used in shipping canned goods and containers for bombs and other munitions. Mr. Fox served as president of the village and as president of the water board. In 1943 high water took out the dam that furnished most of the power to the mill. Then while repairs were being made a flood destroyed all the progress they had made. A fire finally destroyed the mill in 1946.

The next owner of the house was the White family who were related to the Foxs. The White family converted the house into a Bed & Breakfast. In 2000 it was purchased by the Orr family who have updated it. This beautiful building is now the Fox Inn Bed & Breakfast.

160 Main Street (GRL)

Number **160 Main Street** was built in 1880 for Edson and Elizabeth Friend Potter on property which was originally owned by William M. Oliver. Elizabeth was the step-daughter of Peter Oliver, Andrew Oliver's son and William Oliver's nephew. Edson Potter organized the Yates County Lumber Company in 1909. He later added a basket factory to the company. The lumber company held the patent on automatic stapling machines used in the manufacturing of Climax baskets used for grapes and other fruits. Climax baskets were popular because they had a lid and a wood handle. They maintained the quality of the grapes during shipment and were also just the right size for customers. They held a perfect quantity for eating and making jam or jelly.

This house was built in Eastlake style. Take some time to look at the details. Be sure to notice the front gable and the perforated Eastlake designs on the porch posts, the roof brackets, over the windows and elsewhere. The architectural details of this house are indeed special. See the thin cornice brackets, spindle work, and the beautiful paneled front door. Notice the multi-color stone over the windows. Don't miss the oriel window on the north side. The carving, the brick work and the use of many different materials make this house very interesting. It is considered to be high Victorian style. In 1935 it was owned by Arnold James Potter. He lived and died here. Rodney Pierce, Arnold's nephew inherited the property in 1951 when Arnold died. He sold the house to the Elks Lodge in 1955.

Number **162 Main** was built in 1871 in high Italianate style by David B. Prosser, a very successful attorney. He removed the brick house that was located here at the time and occupied by Leander Reddy. David's monogram is carved into the keystone above the front door. This house is an excellent example of how the Italianate style

162 Main Street (GRL)

can be interpreted in masonry. The shape of the tall windows with their curved moldings and large pane glass are repeated in the elegant front door. The portico and cornice are wood. The bay window is also a common feature of Italianate houses. Prosser's parents came to the area with Jemima Wilkinson, the Public Universal Friend. In 1827 Samuel S. Curtiss' second chair manufacturing establishment was located here. Curtiss' home was located behind the factory facing Liberty Street. The property changed hands several times. In 1852 Leander Reddy's wife Rachel owned the property and held a one room private school in one of the extra Curtiss buildings at the back. She sold the property to Maria Prosser, wife of the original builder, in 1870. In 1880 Maria sold the property to Emmet C. Dwelle. He was a wool dealer and served on the village board. In 1882 he helped form the grain merchant company of Sherman, Lewis and Dwelle. Before you leave be sure to look at the carriage house behind the house.

164 Main Street (SM)

Number **164 Main** is an elaborate Italianate shell for a brick gable front Greek Revival house. It was built about 1825 by either Elijah Ryno or Samuel Lawrence. Ryno purchased the property in 1824 and then in 1826 sold it to Samuel Lawrence. At that time it was a brick gable front Greek Revival house. Lawrence was supervisor and a member of the State Assembly in 1818. He was one of those

Looking north with 164 and 166 on the left. The spire of the Penn Yan Methodist Church can be seen in the distance. (YCGHS)

responsible for forming the town of Milo out of part of Benton. In 1821 Governor DeWitt Clinton appointed him sheriff of Ontario County.

In 1844 the house was sold to Leander Reddy by Lawrence's second wife and children. He then sold it back to Polly Lawrence the following year. In 1849 she sold the house to Joseph Elmendorf. The house was sold again in 1863 to Lyman Munger, a druggist and a very active abolitionist. He helped with the Underground Railroad and also supported prohibition.

In 1866 George McAllister, a local builder, bought the property. He made extensive Italianate changes adding the decorative porches and the beautiful elements around the cornices and in the pediment By the end of the century it was owned by William S. Briggs. He studied law with David Prosser who had built the house next door to the south. In 1855 he was county judge. In 1910 Judge William Morris moved the house south and back from the street when he was remodeling the house at 166 Main. The additions at the rear date to 1910. Notice the multiple porches, the heavy brackets and double column posts. These are all typical for Yates County.

The core of **166 Main** Street is a brick house built around 1825 by Ira Gould. About 1857 Myron Hamlin bought 126-128 Main Street for his store, the Metropolitan, which had two previous locations. At the time it was said to be the best store in Penn Yan. Hamlin had been a merchant in Dundee before he came to Penn Yan. He refused to sell liquor in his store, keeping temperance literature on the counter, and including it with every package he made up. His sons continued the Metropolitan after he died. It was located where Henderson Drugs is today.

166 Main Street (GRL)

In the 1850s Henry B. Bennett, who owned a Penn Yan bookstore and was president of the Bank of Bainbridge, owned the house. Hamlin bought it back and sold it again in 1866, this time to attorney Daniel Morris. Morris spent two terms in Congress. William T. Morris inherited the building about 1867. In 1910 the property received major renovations. The original 1825 red brick Federal style house is encased in the middle of this building. Additions were made to both sides and the back. Note the leaded windows. The dormers and the iron work are part of the 1910 addition. The original house was encased in square hollow yellow glazed tiles and then sprayed with stucco transforming it into a house with Classical Revival details. Notice the fan-lighted doorway, the Federal door, the plain two story columns, the pilasters with Ionic capitals and the side porches. In 1927 the house was purchased by H. Allen Wagener. He and his brother had a shoe factory on Central Avenue near the station and owned the first car dealership in Penn Yan. The Methodist Church purchased the building in 1958.

There were alleys which ran behind the houses in the residential district and the businesses in the commercial district. The alley that ran behind these houses led to Curtiss' chair factory. Curtiss sold the right-of-way to the Methodists when he moved.

Number **168 Main Street**, the **Methodist Church**, is an impressive building. The original Penn Yan Methodist church was on the north side of Chapel Street a couple of doors back of the Oliver house. In 1841, a Congregational Church was located here.

The Methodists bought this lot in 1857. In 1872 the Methodists sold their first church on Chapel Street and used some of the money to paint the old Congregational church which was on this lot. In 1896 they decided to build a new church. The corner stone was laid in 1897. The new church was dedicated in January 1898. It cost $35,000 to build. Constructed of red Medina sandstone, it is in a Romanesque Revival style, the model of a medieval fortress. The church is the most magnificent church in Penn Yan. The stained glass windows are original to the building and have been well maintained.

168 Main Street , Penn Yan United Methodist Church, date unknown. (YCGHS)

168 Main Congregationalist's Church Building (PYHist)

In the 1890s Penn Yan was a prosperous village. A lot of that prosperity resulted from the shipping of fresh fruit. The business district was considerably larger than

A postcard of the interior of the Methodist Church. (YCGHS)

it is today because people had more money to spend on housing and other desires. Their prosperity also made it possible to construct this large, beautiful church. In the early 1970s the west wing was taken down and a new education wing was added.

Number **200 Main Street** is transitional Greek Revival and Italianate style strongly influenced by Egyptian Revival. Notice the columns, the windows and the brackets which are close together. The brick was no doubt made locally and would have originally been

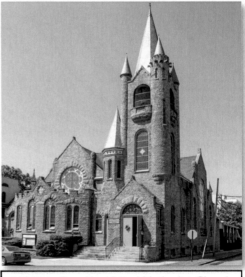

168 Main, Penn Yan United Methodist Church today. (SM)

painted. Before 1824 this lot was vacant. In 1824 a shoemaker named Alexander Hemiup had his shop here. In 1852 Dr. William M. Oliver, Dr. Andrew Oliver's son, got married. Andrew built this house for his son as a wedding gift. In the 1840s before the Olivers purchased

131

200 Main Street, the Oliver House Museum of the Yates County Genealogical and Historical Society (GRL)

the land there was a tavern on the site belonging to Levi Hoyt. The Wesleyan Methodists used the tavern's upper room as their meeting place while they were building their church at 300 Main. The cupola on the roof provided an escape for hot air. With the windows open hot air would rise up the stairs and out helping keep the house cool. The younger Dr. William and his daughters lived here. Dr. Oliver died in 1902. When his last child, daughter Carrie, died in 1942 her will donated the house to the Village of Penn Yan for use as a library, or for historical and museum purposes, along with an endowment to help maintain it. Today it is used by the Yates County Genealogical & Historical Society. You should take time to stop and tour the house, visit the Underwood House and the Jemima Wilkinson exhibit in the carriage house as well. The Society is open Tuesday through Friday.

Number **202 Main Street** was built about 1905. The lot was bought from young Dr. William Oliver. Drs. Andrew Oliver and William once had their office here. In 1902 the land was vacant. The house has an octagonal turret in front, fish scale shingles in the side gables and a double windowed pedimented dormer. The porch

202 Main Street (GRL)

originally wrapped around the front of the building. The style is late Victorian, simpler than the 19th Century Queen Anne style. The property was sold to E. Lynch in 1941.

204 Main Street today (GRL)

The land where number **204 Main** sits was bought from Abraham Wagener in 1818. Dr. Andrew F. Oliver, the twin brother of William Oliver, built a frame house here about 1820. It was often photographed. In 1857, when Dr. Oliver died, his daughter Jane and her husband John L. Lewis, Jr. inherited it. They remodeled it

133

204 Main Street from the 1876 Yates County Atlas

adding a beautiful wrap around porch. It was extensively remodeled in 1902 in this late Victorian style. The house was sold to Charles N. Kelley in 1928. It has never had a lot of decoration. The side porch was added later. It was an attractive single family dwelling. The porch was later reduced and a two-story bay window added to the south side. It was remodeled again in 1935 when the front porch was removed, the east entrance was doubled and a single portico was added. Windows were replaced and the clapboards were covered with shingles.

208 Main Street (GRL)

134

The left image shows the front entry of 208 Main Street. The right image shows the front entry of 328 Main Street. When you look at them next to each other you can clearly see that they are identical. The differences in the colors of their paint make them appear different from a distance.(GRL)

Number **208 Main** has an identical exterior to that of number 328 Main. Lived in by various prosperous Penn Yan merchants, the property was originally sold by Wagener to Abraham H. Bennett in 1824. Bennett was the publisher and editor of the Penn Yan Democrat, one of the two major newspapers in Penn Yan. For a while he printed the paper in a room on the second floor. The present house was remodeled in 1873 by Charles A. Hamlin. Charles was the son of merchant Myron Hamlin who owned the Metropolitan, a dry goods store on Main Street located where Henderson Drug is today. In 1878 he sold the house to George H. Lapham, the founder of the First National Bank of Penn Yan. Lapham was a candidate for State Comptroller in 1882. The bank failed in 1898. Lapham built the carriage house at the back. The house was restored in 1985 and is now the La Belle Vie Bed & Breakfast. The woodwork on the inside is exceptional. Look at the brackets at the cornice, and the moldings above the windows that are pedimented on the second floor and curved on the first. The portico has the same curved moldings. This is a special Italianate house. When you see 328 Main notice how it is identical to this house. You will also notice how different they appear due to the differences in paint color.

The property for number **210 Main Street** was once A. H Bennett's print shop. Elisha G. Hopkins built his house here in

1844. He built his cabinet making shop and office on the site where the present library sits. In 1899 a new home was built here. Notice the Doric columns on the porch and the strong Classic Revival influence. At some point someone replaced the siding and stripped the house of it's decorative trim. It doesn't look much like it did originally.

210 Main Street (GRL)

214 Main Street, old postcard (YCGHS)

214 Main Street, the **Penn Yan Library**. In 1827 Abraham sold this lot to Elisha Hopkins for his business. The early beginnings of the library date back to 1833 when a group of young men formed the Washington Club. They brought speakers, such as Ralph Waldo Emerson and Horace Greeley, to Penn Yan. The club incorporated in 1842 so that they could conduct a public library. In 1857 a new group of young businessmen formed the Penn Yan Lyceum. Then in 1884 38 people formed the Library Club. They provided books to the Penn Yan

214 Main Street today (GRL)

Academy for a library. On June 6, 1895 the Penn Yan Board of Education made the library public with a 5 member board of trustees. In 1899 the library's hours were 4 to 6 p.m. weekdays and 7 to 9pm on Saturdays.

In 1903 the Penn Yan School District authorized the acceptance of a $10,000 Andrew Carnegie grant to build a library building. Carnegie donated more than 40 million dollars between 1886 and 1919 to pay for 1679 libraries. He was a great philanthropist, giving away almost 90% of his fortune. In 1904 some interested citizens donated $3000 to purchase the site. The 70 foot wide lot on Main Street was purchased from Elisha Hopkins. Hopkins once had a sawmill with cabinet manufacturing and coffin sales there. The library opened to the public in June 1905. It has a Neoclassical facade with a central pedimented porch, full height Tuscan columns and brick pilasters. The window molding and deep entablature are reminders of its Greek Revival inspirations. The new addition at the back of the building was kept low to blend in. Notice the interior muntins on the windows.

218 Main Street, no longer exists (HP)

218 Main Street was once located where you now find the driveway for the new County buildings. It was torn down in 2002. It was likely built about 1828 by Ebenezer Brown. He bought the property from William Tolford, who had purchased it from Abraham Wagener in 1824. Brown was Penn Yan's postmaster. William M. Oliver bought it in 1836 and sold it to Charles Judd, an attorney. He was appointed to the position of district attorney in 1836 and served till 1841. The house was originally built in Greek Revival style. Two porches and two wings were added to the house making it look more Italianate.

224 Main Street – the **First Baptist Church**. By 1834 this land belonged to Ebenezer Brown who sold it to the trustees of the

Church. Before the church was built the congregation met in the old schoolhouse on Liberty Street, then in the Masonic Lodge on Court Street. In 1831 they began meeting in the Court House where they remained until it burned in 1834. This building stands on the same ground as the first Baptist Church built here in 1835 of brick in the Greek Revival style.

Postcard of the First Baptist Church (YCGHS)

138

224 Main Street (GRL)

It was smaller than the current one. The second church on the site was completed in 1871. At that time it had the tallest steeple in the village, 120 feet high. It would sway in a strong wind. Structural problems resulted in its removal and the current steeple was added later. Note the unusual cube on the top — it is an uncommon religious symbol and stands for God the Father. This is the oldest active church building in Penn Yan. The brick was sand blasted in the 1970s. Around 1985 the brick, which had been damaged by the sand blasting, was restored.

Postcard of the First Baptist Church interior (YCGHS)

County Government Buildings. The **Court House** was built in 1835 by Enoch Bordwell. The price of the two acres that the county buildings sit on were listed at a consideration of $5,000 on the deed to the county by Abraham Wagener. Wanting to bring the county seat to Penn Yan, he believed it was important for there to be a place for the county offices. The Court House yard was

County Court House (1835) and County Office Building (1889) (YCGHS)

Postcard of the back of the Court House and County Office Building, date unknown
(YCGHS)

"New" Jail on Liberty Street (YCGHS)

originally so wet that there was standing water where huge bull frogs lived. It was drained so that the area was able to be used for public gatherings. The annual Agricultural Fair was held here from 1840 until 1851. At the beginning of the Civil War, when the Keuka Rifles left Penn Yan for Elmira, residents gathered in front of the court house to hear speeches from local dignitaries. The yard used to be surrounded by a wrought iron fence which was taken down during WW II for the iron.

The third Jail, a replacement for the "New" Jail (YCGHS)

The **original court house** was built in 1824. It included a two cell jail and was burned down by a prisoner in 1834. It was rebuilt a year later at a cost of $12,000. This Greek Revival building looks like the old one; however, it is larger and does not include a jail. The village built a separate jail which included a residence for the sheriff. It was a stucco covered stone building and faced Liberty Street. There is a cupola on top of the court house with a bell which was rung when court was in session.

The Old County Court House today (GRL)

In 1835, the **county clerk's** office was built next to the Court House. It was a small building built of stone with a pillared portico. Considered to be fire proof, it also stored the county's records.

The **new jail** on Liberty Street burned in 1857. It was replaced by a third jail built in 1906; the present one, built in 1974, is in the County Safety Building. In 1889 a new county office building replaced the county clerk's office. The new building was brick with stone arches in Richardsonian style. It is still standing and in use. In 2002 the new county office building was built and attached to the 1956 and 1968 additions to the 1889 county office building and the court house. The new court house facing Liberty Street was erected at the same time.

The **Soldiers & Sailor Monument** was erected in 1908 as a Civil War memorial. The population of the county at the time of the war was 20,290 and the number who enlisted was 2,109 – over 10% of the population and 40% of those eligible. The base of the monument is 24 feet, 6 inches square and weighs an estimated 120 tons. The four figures are each six feet, four inches tall. The slender shaft includes the names of the principal battles of the Civil War in which men from Yates County fought – Gettysburg, Fredericksburg,

The County Office Building and the Soldiers & Sailors Monument. Note the Civil War cannons and stacked cannon balls. (YCGHS)

Wilderness, Antietam, Petersburg, Spotsylvania and Appomatox. The color bearer at the top of the monument represents the color guard of the 126th New York who fought at the Wheatfield in the battle of Gettysburg. There used to be huge civil war naval cannons surrounding the monument. Metal was needed in World War II so the cannons were taken to be melted down. The current band stand was put up in 1998. In 1888 one was located where the monument stands today. It was moved in 1908 to the south side of the central sidewalk, near where the present one stands today.

Number **300 Main Street** is the oldest remaining religious structure in Penn Yan. Naturally, the lot originally belonged to Abraham Wagener. He sold it in 1823, shortly after he provided land for the county office buildings. Built about 1851 by the Methodist seceders, it was used until 1864 when the war ended and the congregation reunited. The Methodists were just one of several religious groups that split over the abolition movement. It wasn't that people were pro-slavery. Most Democrats were in favor of states rights and did not believe that the government should interfere with slavery, nor should people break the law. Notice the double Doric pilasters on the front. The doorway is Greek Revival. The porch on the south side is new. The trim was originally white and the body color a light yellow. The long narrow garage on the side street used to be a horse shed.

300 Main Street (GRL)

In 1855 this was the site of a women's rights convention. Organizers of the event were Mrs. Stafford C. Cleveland and Mrs. Abner Bridgman. The convention was modeled after the convention in Seneca Falls held in 1848. Speakers included Susan B. Anthony from Rochester and Ernestine L. Rose from New York City. Susan dedicated her life to the abolition of slavery and woman suffrage. She defied the Fugitive Slave Act and worked with Harriet Tubman on the Underground Railroad. She was one of the leaders of the Seneca Falls Convention and a co-author of *History of Woman Suffrage*. Ernestine was one of America's first female speakers for women's rights. She supported a law that gave New York women the right to own property.

In 1864 Henry Bradley and Eliza Heerman bought the building and converted it into a boarding house which Eliza ran for almost 10 years. Next it became a single family residence. In 1946 it was owned by Sheriff Mervin Rapalee and his wife. It was conveniently located close to the jail. Previous sheriffs lived in the jail. Since Rapalee's home was so close to the jail he felt he could live at home. While he was in office six prisoners managed to escape by putting a hole through the brick wall. Perhaps had he lived in the jail this would not have happened, but we will never know that for sure. The building now contains apartments.

304 Main Street was built in 1868 by Perley Curtiss, Samuel Curtiss' son, shortly after he got married. Perley was a partner with W. H. Fox in the Fox Paper Mill. He was also part of the syndicate that started the Penn Yan Railway Company along the Outlet. In 1882 Curtiss transferred the house to George Olmstead. It is a fine example of Second Empire architecture.

304 Main Street (GRL)

Number **306 Main Street** was built by Judge Henry Wells in 1831. Wells bought the lot from John Rumney in 1830. Around 1819 the property was occupied by Amasa Holden, a maker of high quality furniture. Holden and his oldest son both volunteered at the beginning of the War of 1812. He was a fifer and his son a drummer boy. Holden's cabinet making shop was the first in the village. In 1888 Hanford and Laura Struble bought the property. He was district attorney from 1869 till 1872. He served in the State Assembly from 1874 to 1875. Then in 1883 till 1889 he was County Judge and Surrogate. The house

306 Main Street today (GRL)

is a transition style, a hybrid between Federal and Greek Revival. Today it has a classic temple front in the Greek Revival style. The porch on the side is 20th century Classical Revival. The entablature and pediment have some very fine dentil work.

306 Main Street. Hon. Henry Wells residence from 1857 Penn Yan map (YCH)

308 Main Street (GRL)

Number **308 Main Street**. Laura Struble sold this lot to Edward Donahue in 1899. He then sold it to Margaret Dewan. The house is an example of the trend to make Queen Anne style homes simpler.

Originally a commercial lot, number **310 Main**

Street's lot was split in the 1840s. The property was owned by Martin B. Lewis, son of schoolmaster John L. Lewis, Sr., in 1857. James Armstrong purchased the lot that same year. It is likely that he built this house before he sold off the lot and built the house next door. In

310 Main (GRL)

1869 extensive renovations were made to the house by Henry Douglas. It is a modest Italianate in style.

Number **312 Main.** In 1815 this was Asa Cole's property. It changed hands many times. James Armstrong bought it in 1866 from Ephraim Whitaker. Armstrong, the hardware king, built this house that same year. He was part of the Armstrong & Gage hardware store which in 1861 was

312 Main Street (GRL)

located where Pinckney Hardware is today. This was once a commercial lot. Joseph Vansandt and George Hanford had a store here in 1819. Armstrong built number 310 first. He lived there while he built number 312. Once 312 was completed, he moved. This house is Italianate Victorian. The decorative brackets, bay windows, pediments and a wonderful porch are worthy of note. Be sure to also note the carriage house in the back with the beautiful cupola.

312 Main Street Carriage House (GRL)

Number **314 Main Street** is the current middle school athletic field. It sat on two acres that Abraham Wagener sold to Dr. Dorman in 1804. Dorman's widow sold it to Frederick Rohde, a shoemaker, and his wife Elizabeth Dean. Her father was an early settler. Before 1806 the Rohdes built a house here and set aside part of the lot for a school. School Master John

Penn Yan Middle School athletic field on site of 314 Main Street (GRL)

L. Lewis, Sr. was a teacher there in 1815. The school became the building where the first religious meetings were held. The Methodists met there shortly after 1800. They were the first group of Methodists in western New York. The Presbyterians also met there while their church was being built. Hugh Joynt married the Rohdes' daughter and went to Oil City, Pennsylvania during the 1865 oil rush. There was a small building on the property that held gun powder for a while. In 1857 Rohde sold the property to Charles V. Bush who built the old Academy here. The school was enlarged significantly in 1905 and finally a new Junior High School was built in 1928. The Academy was razed in 1965 to make room for athletic fields.

322 Main Street (YCH)

322 Main Street. Melatiah Lawrence had a house on the site in 1822. Jonathan Hall purchased the property in 1838. He sold it to Cornelius Masten. When Masten died in 1842 it became a part of his estate and was needed to pay his debts. A lawsuit resulted which was not settled until 1855. The plaintiff Geneva lawyer, Joseph Fellows, finally sold the property to Maria Brown in 1862. Interestingly, Maria, wife of Morris Brown, had been living in the home since 1857. During the lawsuit William S. Briggs occupied the home. He had enlarged it adding two wings, a second story and a new roof and turning the house into an Italianate style mansion with a large front porch and a cupola. When Maria died the house passed to her brother-in-law who returned it to Morris Brown. Nelson Thompson acquired the house in 1883 as payment for debts. He in turn sold it to John Gulick from Elmira. The next owner was Ruth Griggs. In 1955 it was willed to the library who sold it to the Penn Yan Civic Center. Since that use could not be justified the school district razed the building.

Number **326 Main** was built on a vacant lot about 1883 by John G. Gulick of Elmira. It's a restrained Victorian which has lost some of its ornamentation. The property was part of Nelson Thompson's estate. Thompson had a livery stable in Penn Yan and a meat market. In 1892 it was inherited by John H. Johnson, president of Citizens Bank. The Johnson family owned it till 1960.

326 Main Street (GRL)

Number 328 is identical to number 208. However, with the building painted all in white you cannot help but notice how the details fade into the background. It was probably built by Charles C. Sheppard in 1868. He was the first Morris Sheppard's youngest son. Charles was a member of Penn Yan's first Board of Education from 1857 to 1874. He was its president for 9 years. He was a delegate to the Republican National Convention that nominated

328 Main Street (GRL)

Abraham Lincoln in 1860. Sheppard contributed to the building of the Presbyterian Church in the 1870s and was a strong member of the congregation. His wife was Jane Bradley, daughter of merchant Henry Bradley, abolition and temperance advocate. It is an elaborate Italianate style. James Grieve's store was on this site in 1823 when Henry Bradley took it over. It was moved across the street when 328 was built. Sheppard sold the property to Reuben Scofield in 1880. His family kept it until 1923. He was the editor of the Penn Yan Express newspaper for many years.

Number **330 Main** is a mix of styles. Notice the Italianate features. The portico was once a front porch. Known as the Leary

House, it was likely built in 1868 by Charles C. Sheppard's son Morris F. Sheppard on land that was previously commercial property. In 1823 it was Henry Bradley's store. His house on North Avenue, gone now, was a station on the underground railroad. Bradley was a strong supporter of temperance and abolition. In 1846 he ran for Governor of New York on the Liberty

330 Main Street (GRL)

Party. In 1877 the house was sold to Michael Leary, whose wife was one of the Sheppard grandchildren. Especially noteworthy are the brackets in the gables, the arched windows and the east portico. The cupola is much smaller than it was originally.

332 Main Street, Emmuanel Baptist Church (GRL)

Number **332 Main** was once a house built in 1871 by John S. Sheppard, son of Charles C. Sheppard. The structure was a two and a half story mansion with a mansard roof built in

338 Main Street (GRL)

second Empire style. Nelson Damoth's family bought it in 1909. The house was torn down when the Emmanuel Baptist church was built here in 1961.

338 Main Street was built by Dr. Francis M. Potter in 1832 on land he purchased from Morris Sheppard. In 1840 he sold it to Morris Sheppard's son, Charles, who lived next door. Charles' daughter sold it to George R. Cornwell in 1905. This building was originally Greek Revival in style. Notice the double leaf door which was typical of Penn Yan architecture at the time. The moldings around the windows are Greek Revival as are the pilasters on the corners. Sheppard remodeled it in 1855 changing the style to Italianate and making it more elaborate. Changes included the south wing, the brackets and the front entrance. At one time a porch, removed in 1931, ran across the front of the house. The southeast portico, handrail and the main entrance and hand rail replaced the porch. The west wing porch was added in the late 19th century. The addition to the west side of the south wing and the picture window were added at the same time. There are apartments in the back, but the front is a single family home.

342 Main Street is a very beautiful stone house. It was built in 1830 by Morris F. Sheppard in a simple Classic Greek Revival style. Morris Sheppard was an early Penn Yan settler. He came in 1801 and married a sister of David Wagener's wife. His first home was a log cabin along Jacob's Brook. It was also a tannery. He fought against the British at Sodus in the War of 1812. In 1818 he had a gristmill

151

342 Main Street (GRL)

342 Main Street (GRL)

on Sucker Brook in a gulley where he also had a small quarry. He partnered with Nathaniel Higby and Elijah Haskill in a fulling mill (where woven cloth is cleaned and finished) located on Jacob's Brook near the North Avenue bridge. At one time Sheppard owned almost all of the land on both sides of Main Street south of Head Street in the northeast quarter of Lot 37. From 1828 to 1830 he represented Penn Yan in the Assembly.

In 1824, wanting to keep the commercial district at the north end of Main Street, he built a commercial building called Sheppard's Mechanics Hall on this site. It was a large five story wooden building and contained various small shops of artisans, legal offices and perhaps some living quarters. On the upper floor was a lodge room used by the Vernon Chapter 190 F & A Masons. It burned down in December 1826.

Sheppard then built his third and final home on this lot. The stone came from his quarry. Sheppard died in 1846. When his widow died attorney David B. Prosser acquired the house. Prosser sold it to Jarvis Andrews, who in turn sold it to Jeptha Potter in 1871. In 1878 Potter remodeled the house making it more Victorian Italianate in style. Potter removed a portico with columns in the front, replacing it with a small Italianate porch. It is likely that he enlarged the windows at the front on the first floor and added the wooden lintels. Brackets were added under the eaves and he broke up the roof with the gable window. This is one of only two stone houses in Penn Yan. The other stone house is at the west end of Court Street on Highland Drive where Abraham Wagener was living when he died.

344 Main Street (GRL)

344 Main Street. Jeptha Potter who owned the house to the south also owned this lot. He sold it to Edward Berry who built this home in 1898. The architecture is typical of a large three story home of that time. The square tower is unusual, but original. Note the stained glass windows and the detail above the bay and tower windows. Balustrades have been removed above the east

344 Main Street (GRL)

porch, the east bay window, and the flat top roof between the four posts on the tower. The enclosed porch on the west side was added. This house is basically Queen Anne style. The Berrys remained here until the 1920s when Jerome D. Rogers of Roenke & Rogers, a large Penn Yan department store located at 133-141 Main Street, purchased the property.

Number **346 Main Street**. Originally part of the commercial district this lot may have once held Morris F. Sheppard's second home, a one and a half story yellow house which burned in 1846. Stafford C. Cleveland, editor of the Chronicle Express newspaper and author of the book *History of Yates County, New York*, believed this house was built in the 1850s by James Cooley who worked at the

153

346 Main Street (GRL)

Birdsall Iron Works. The Iron Works was located on the north side of Head Street. They built threshers and other equipment. Cooley came from Ireland. A map shows Henry Hubbard living here in 1857. He sold it to Elizabeth Cooley in 1859.

This house was first an L shaped Greek Revival. Edmund Bowers remodeled it in 1868 to Italianate style making the pilasters more elaborate. It was remodeled again in 1916 by John C. Fox who converted it to a Colonial Revival style. Before this remodel it had at least three porches with ogee brackets. Notice the elaborate pilasters, the beautiful porch and the triple windows. The windows are 20th century.

Number 348 was built in 1906 by Clinton Struble. the prominent attorney who owned the Arcade building on Main Street, on a lot that had once been commercial with inns and stores. It is a simple frame house. The porch was more common to houses built during the late 19th Century. This house is Early Classic Revival. Note the pattern in the glass of the porch window. Morris F. Sheppard owned all this land at one time.

348 Main Street (GRL)

350 Main Street. Originally this was part of the commercial district. This corner lot was part of the 2 acres that Morris Sheppard sold to Abner Pierce in 1805. Pierce then sold the corner to Samuel Seeley and William Baldwin. They built the first store in the village. It is said that when Robert Chissom died in 1806, Pierce ran a tavern here. The store

350 Main Street (GRL)

was sold to Ezra Rice in 1809, who ran it as a tavern. Early taverns were a place where you could obtain food and drink as well as some staple goods. Of course they also provided a place for travelers to stay the night. In 1810 Rice sold the property to Joel Dorman. Asa Cole had a tavern across Head Street and stores filled both the southeast and southwest corners. Periodically fires caused buildings to be rebuilt. Around 1832 William and John Brooks built a block of stores which managed to last until 1846. Henry Bradley had a store here in 1833. It was sold to Charles Sheppard in 1834. In 1840 Francis M. Potter bought the property and replaced it with a block of stores across the street. In 1846 there was another fire. Birdsall bought the corner in 1860 after it had once again been destroyed by fire. He built his manufacturing business. Birdsall's factory remained until the early 1900s when another fire destroyed the property and allowed William Comstock to put in a grocery store which lasted until the 1880s. William N. Wise bought the lot and built 350 in 1906. He never lived here; he built the house as an investment and sold it to Harriet Mosher in 1907. It is a simple frame house. Now cross over North Avenue to the east side of Main Street.

355-361 Main Street, Penn Yan Area Volunteer Ambulance Corp (GRL)

The Ambulance Corps has been located here at **355-361 Main** Street since 1972. This was the first cross roads in Penn Yan and the location of the first firehouse in

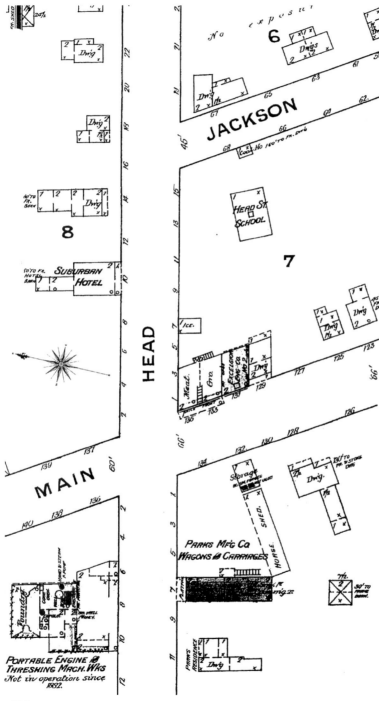

Detail from the 1886 Sanborn Map #7 showing the Main and Head Street area. You can see where some businesses, the firehouse and the Head Street School were once located. Note that North arrow is to the left.

the village. In 1790 Head Street as it was called then (now North Avenue), went east to Hopeton and Geneva, and west up Widow Hill to Canandaigua. In 1791 Robert Chissom, George Wheeler's son-in-law, lived a block to the west (See map on page 6.) The northeast corner was where William Babcock lived. There was a store there in the early 1800s. This was the village. Asa Cole had a tavern and stage stop at the northwest corner. It wasn't until 1799 that Main Street went from here to the mills.

This land was part of the 20 acres sold by Abraham Wagener to John W. Hedges in 1814. As you are aware Abraham inherited much of Penn Yan when his father died in 1799. In 1824 the property was sold to John VanPelt. This was the location of the commercial district. Penn Yan's first store was the first building to be located here. It was in business for a year or two when Luman Phelps bought it. He turned it into a tavern. Behind it,

359-361 Main Street. Built by Henry Carley in 1869. He had his meat market on 1st floor and apartments above. The fire station is to the right. (PYH)

facing North Avenue (formerly Head Street), was the village's first firehouse. It burned down. Next to it was the Head Street schoolhouse in 1886, still there in 1903 but unused. Around 1911 the schoolhouse became a Fundamentalist Methodist church complete with a steeple. It was razed in 1972. The Red Building, which contained stores, was destroyed in a fire in 1831. In 1869 Henry Carley built a brick double store with his meat market one of the two. Engine House #2 was next door. (See map on page 156)

Number 351. Notice the stone foundation. The house standing here now was built about 1842 by Henry Bradley. In 1818 the property was sold by Nehemiah Higley, a partner of Morris F. Sheppard in the fulling mill, to Cornelius Masten. Masten in turn sold it to George Youngs who immediately sold it to Henry Bradley. Bradley came to Penn Yan in 1823 and rented a store which was also used as his

351 Main Street (GRL)

349 Main Street (GRL)

home. After a year he bought William Babcock's store at the northeast corner of Head Street. He eventually became partners with Charles C. Sheppard. In the 1840s they moved their businesses downtown and built five store fronts on the west side of Main Street. In 1857 when this property was sold to Ebenezer Lewis there was a small white house on the lot which may have once been a store. Bradley owned several stores which he rented out to various businessmen. The dormers and the front porch are all new.

349 Main was a blacksmith shop and a residence owned by Franklin A. Risdon in the 1830s. Risdon sold the property to James S. Powell in 1862. He sold it to Michael Mahon in 1864. It was built in the Italianate style, but was very plain. The portico is early 20th century. At the northeast corner of Main and Head Streets (now North Avenue) was the Carriage works. At the northwest corner Birdsall sold agricultural equipment.

345 Main Street (GRL)

The present **345 Main** property was owned by James A. MacKellar in 1886. This house was built about 1925 by Parmalee Johnson. A local historian and a banker, he wanted his home to look like it was built in 1825, Federal style. It is a good adaptation. There was great attention to detail when it was built. Note the detail on the pilasters, the cornice and around the portico. The 3 fold windows, the porch and dormer may have been added later in the 20th century.

Number 343 was the MacKellar house. The land was part of Morris F. Sheppard's property in 1812 and it may have been the site

343 Main Street (GRL)

of Sheppard's original 1801 log cabin and tannery. In 1868 it was owned by Mary Parks. In 1886 it was sold to James MacKellar. The house has had extensive modernization. The only architectural details that remain are the lancet windows and the fish scale woodwork in the gables.

Number **341 Main** was owned by Morris F. Sheppard. His first log home, built in 1801, was located either here or next door. He gave the cabin to Keziah Sabin when her husband died and her daughter married Frederick Pierce. This stucco bungalow was built in the 1920s by Isaac Yetter. He was part of Kinne & Yetter. They handled coal, wood, and a line of materials for masons. Their business was so large that they had a

341 Main Street (GRL)

159

branch on Bluff Point. He moved the old house north of Head Street. Notice the deep roof, the porch and the dormers. This shows the influence of Frank Lloyd Wright. There is beautiful craftsman's style woodwork inside.

337 Main Street. This lot belonged to Morris F. Sheppard in 1814. He sold it to William Babcock who sold it to Elijah Spencer in 1824. He sold it to Morris

337 Main Street (SM)

Earle in 1830. Earle was a tailor who had his shop and residence adjacent to the lot. He rented out this house and in 1856 sold the property to Stephen Raymond who sold this portion of the lot to Mary Jane Landon in 1863. It is a simple Italianate style. Be sure to note the small porch on the south, now an entry, which has a different style support than the large porch on the west side. The west porch may have replaced an earlier one.

333 Main Street. The front part of this house was probably built by John VanPelt Jr., a soldier in the War of 1812, about 1824. This land also once belonged to Morris F. Sheppard. Notice the Federal proportions. The portico is 20th century. The back part of the house may date to as early as 1814. If so, it is the oldest house in Penn Yan. In 1804 Dr. Dorman bought the lot from Abraham Wagener. It was sold to Dr. William Cornwell in 1815. He sold it to John VanPelt in 1824. The back house and the front house were likely separate for some time. When they were joined we do not know. In 1842 it was owned by Charles and Sarah Scott. He was a jeweler from London with a shop on Head Street. It has five fireplaces — two downstairs, two upstairs

333 Main Street (GRL)

333 Main Street rear detail (GRL)

and a large cooking fireplace with a bake oven at the back of the
house in the old section. Imagine early residents cooking there. The
windows were all hand made, 12 over 12s on the lower floor and 12
over 8s on the second floor. The woodwork is marvelous. The stairway
is made of cherry. The old part of the building may have once stood
on the lot of number 337. Mill Street, once a private road, at one
time went to the fulling mill on Jacob's Brook. It may also have gone
down to Morris Sheppard's tannery. This is one of the most important
historic structures in Penn Yan.

331 Main Street (SM)

331 Main was G. Fred Wagener's home, built early in 1896. He was H. Allen Wagener's brother. They operated a shoe factory in Penn Yan in 1901. The factory was located behind the Sheppard Opera House for a couple of years. Then they built a larger factory on Seneca Street at the corner of Central Avenue. They had a shoe store on Main Street that carried only the best shoes and boots. In 1903, they also owned the first car dealership in Penn Yan; it was located on East Elm across from the Sampson Theatre. The house is a wonderful example of late Queen Anne style. Notice the deep porch with swag detailed railing, the asymmetrical massing, the leaded section on the upper part of the windows, the doric columns on the porch and the paneled chimney. The house looks very much as it did when it was first built.

327 Main Street, south side (GRL)

327 Main Street, north side (SM)

327 Main Street, south side (GRL)

Number **327 Main** is a single family home. Prior to 1818 it was owned by a lawyer, the first district attorney Abraham P. Vosburgh. He was a prominent attorney and became the County's first surrogate judge. The south half was built first and then in 1851 Cornelius Masten, attorney of law, decided to add the second half. It was built to match. On the outside it is a very symmetrical house, both halves match. However, on the inside while the addition's window locations match, the floors do not. It is timber framed and the foundation to the north is cobblestone. It has the same under eaves decoration, Egyptian Revival, as the Oliver House located at 200 Main Street. The front porch is 20th century. The additions to the rear were made by John H. Butler, publisher of "The Vineyardist" and a grape grower. The Vineyardist was a semi-monthly journal "devoted to the interests of fruit growers." On the vacant lot next door there was a house, 329 Main, lived in by General Claude Ferenbaugh which burned down about 25 years ago.

Number **325 Main** Street was built in 1815. This is one of the oldest remaining houses in Penn Yan. Dr. William Cornwell Jr. bought the lot from Dr. Dorman shortly after he was married. A few years later he bought a 5 acre lot which stretched from around number 311 Main to the Court Street Extension. Dr. Cornwell did not practice medicine very long.

325 Main Street (GRL)

He became deputy sheriff of Ontario County and was Colonel of the Penn Yan Regiment of Militia in the 103rd infantry regiment. From 1820 through 1821 he represented Ontario County in the Assembly. He clerked for attorney William M. Oliver in 1820 and was licensed as an attorney in 1829. His youngest son, George R. Cornwell owned the Cornwell Opera House where Longs' Cards and Books is located today.

The house belonged to Dr. Charles B. Scudder in 1925 when it changed from a vernacular Federal style house to the Dutch Revival gambrel roof home you see today. Many doctors have lived here. The next owner was Dr. Bernard Strait. It was then sold to Dr. Wilfred McCusker. The front entrance is Federal style as are the pilasters on the ends. The triple windows, the second floor, the attic and the portico are all 20th century.

323 Main (GRL)

321 Main (GRL)

Numbers 323 and 321. This land once belonged to Dr. William Cornwell. 321 was built in 1936 by Henry Putnam, but the foundation dates back to the 19th century when the parsonage for the Methodist Church was located here. Number 323 was built in 1921 by Jared A. Darrow. He sold it to William N. Wise in 1927. Wise who was the grape king, part owner of the hardware store Hollowell & Wise, as well as the Fuel Administrator for Yates County during WWI led the group that was instrumental in the creation of Soldiers & Sailors Memorial Hospital. He deeded the property to the hospital who owned it till 1954.

Numbers 319 and 317 are located where the original St. Mark's Episcopal Church stood in 1838. This property was sold by the church

319 Main Street (GRL)

317 Main Street (GRL)

319 Main before 1917 (Wolcott)

when abolition caused a split in the congregation. William N. Wise bought the whole lot. He built 319 Main in 1879. Wise made much of his money shipping grapes by rail. He sold the land where number 317 is located to Arthur Jessup in 1880. Jessup was a harness maker with a shop on Elm Street. 317 is Victorian in style, has a Classic Revival window with leaded glass and a paneled chimney. There used to be a porch on the northwest corner. Fred Hollowell later lived in 319. He served in the State Legislature for 30 years. Number 319 was originally built in Eastlake style. Notice the oriel window on the north side, the paneled brick chimney, and the front windows which are set at a diagonal. Unfortunately much of the character was lost when the clapboard was covered over.

315 Main Street (GRL)

Number **315 Main Street** was built about 1844 by widow Lucy Wilber or by John J. Rosenbury. Rosenbury did own the property after Lucy. He was a law partner of attorney John Tuttle Andrews. The house is Greek Revival. Since it was

165

315 Main Street (GRL)

built without an architect, it is simple in design. Notice the temple front and the unique square posts rather than the usual columns. It is possible that there may have been two additions on the east side of the house. The second story screened porch on the north end also appears to be an addition. For a while it was rented as a temporary residence for a number of Presbyterian and Episcopal clergy.

Number 311. The center of this house was Dr. William Cornwell's second home. Dr. Cornwell was a surgeon in the War of

311 Main Street (GRL)

1812. A prominent man in the early days of Penn Yan, he was both a doctor and a lawyer. This house may have been built in 1819. After Dr. Cornwell died, it was remodeled into the Italianate style. The remodel was likely done in 1863 by George R. Cornwell, Dr. Cornwell's youngest son. He lived here with his mother Sarah for many years. George owned Denton's Book Store on the west side of Main Street which later became Cornwell Books. He also owned the Cornwell Opera House. In 1888, after Sarah died, the third floor was added, the front porch was enlarged and the house was modified into a Queen Anne mansion. The Cornwell family owned this house until 1926 when it was purchased by M. S. Lounsbury.

There was once a one and a half story Greek Revival cottage where number **309 Main** stands today. It was Dr. Cornwell's law office. Later his son in law, Justus S. Glover used the building as both his law office and his residence. In 1853 portrait artist William Linsley lived here. The next owner was James D. Morgan who lived here for some time. In 1894 George S. Sheppard bought the property and

309 Main Street (GRL)

moved the house around the corner to Jackson Street. It was located at the Penn Yan Gas Light Company property when it was torn down to make way for NYSEG. The current 309 was built by Henry C. Underwood in 1909. When he died in 1928 it was sold to Clarence Andrews. It is a good example of Georgian Revival. Notice the carriage house in the back which was added about 1929. The Ionic columns also have Ionic capitals which are unusual in a Georgian Revival house. Also of note are the dentils under the eaves and the Corinthian pilasters. Other interesting features include the Victorian front porch, the pedimented front on the dormer and the palladian windows on the north side.

307 and 305 Main were built about the same time. The Presbyterian meeting house stood here in 1824 on land given to them by Dr. William Cornwell and Henry Plympton. Henry

307 Main Street (GRL)

Bradley gave a speech about temperance here on July 4th, 1826. It was so inspiring that the Yates Republican newspaper published an extra edition to include it. The meeting house was the first in Penn Yan and was located here for over 50 years. A new church was built at Main and Clinton Streets in 1879. The Presbyterians sold the land to Charles D. Welles. Dentist Dr. Herbert MacNaughton bought the property in 1909 and built his home here. Note the patterned decoration in the west gable. The porch, three stories and steeply pitched roof are common features of this time period. It is a very classic early 20th century house.

305 Main Street (GRL)

305 Main. This lot was a part of the one to the north where the meeting house stood. Charles D. Welles built this home in 1883. It's a good example of Victorian Gothic Eastlake style. Note the ornate woodwork in the gables. The mansard roof on the square tower is French Renaissance style. Be sure to notice the rich surface detail.

Number 303 was originally a Federal Style house built in the 1820s by Israel Brown. It was added to and redecorated. Notice the Italianate style porches and the square tower which were added. Be sure to look at the half moon end louvres. The front door is Federal style, asymmetrical with Italianate molding. In 1829 Robert Beecher owned this building which spent some time as a hotel with a temperance bar. It was the only temperance bar in Penn Yan. Without much public support, it did not

303 Main Street GRL)

last long. In 1855, Delancy and Caroline Martin owned the house. It was later owned by Farley Holmes, steamboat captain and president of Keuka Lake Navigation Company. The steamer "Holmes" was named after him.

301 Main Street (GRL)

301 Main Street was built in 1885 by Theodore F. Wheeler, the druggist who owned Wheeler's Drugs once located at 100 Main. This land was purchased from Caroline Martin in 1868. Notice the double door at the front, the trim, numerous stained glass windows, the Gothic tower, the oriel window, the lovely porches and the many different materials used. This house is one of the finest examples of Queen Anne style in the county. The carriage house at the rear is now a house. The property in this section belonged to Israel Brown. His house was on the larger lot that 303 stands on today. The lot once went from Main Street to Jackson Street.

Number **227 Main Street** is the **Yates County Public Safety Building**. Built in 1977, it has a jail with room for 43 prisoners. In 1824 this was the site of Captain Eliah Holcomb's three story Washington House hotel and tavern. Holcomb was an ex sea

227 Main Street when it was a private residence. Ebenezer Jones purchased the original building on the site in 1842. Jones dismantled that building and built this home. After several owners, Walter Wagner bought the house and turned it into the Wagner Hotel in 1932. (YCH)

227 Main Street, The Wagner Hotel after 1932 (YCGHS)

captain from Washington County, New York. He bought about two acres of land from Jonathan Bordwell. In 1829 Dr. Oliver P. Wolcott took over and the building became a schoolhouse, the Yates Academy

227 Main Street, Yates County Public Safety Building (GRL)

and Female Seminary. It remained in business until 1842 when it was purchased by Ebenezer Jones, a Penn Yan merchant. He dismantled the old structure moving the frame to Court House Park where it was used in the construction of the jail barn. Jones built a fabulous residence on the property.

Mrs. Hebe P. Ellsworth, wife of Samuel Stewart Ellsworth, owned it next. In 1877 Charles C. Sheppard bought the property. Then it was owned by Oscar Murray. John Sheppard owned it for a while. In 1932 Walter Wagner turned the property into the Wagner Hotel. The hotel had an Italianate cupola. There was a wrought iron fence around the whole property, and a pavilion in the back. The land went all the way down to Jacob's Brook. It was very elegant — many weddings were held there. It was taken over by the Kicklers in 1949. Then in 1968 the property was purchased by Everett Jensen. In 1971 the building was torn down to make way for the Yates County Public Safety Building that you see here now.

223-225 Main Street, Lake Keuka Floral Company showroom (Wolcott)

171

223-225 Main Street, Brundage greenhouses (Wolcott)

223-225 Main Street before 2012 renovation (GRL)

223-225 Main Street, the new 2012 Flour Shop Cafe and Bakery (GRL)

A double lot number **223 - 225 Main** Street's first owner after Abraham Wagener was a hatter named Joseph Jones, an early settler. Gilbert and Bales acquired the property in 1837. Stephen Gilbert, his wife and son, and John Bales, a bachelor built their home here. It was also used as the Gilbert & Bales' gun factory. They made good quality shotguns. The Gilberts' son, John Gilbert, continued to make guns until they became mass produced so that it was no longer a profitable enterprise. The shotguns made by the Gilberts are collectors' items today.

In 1912 a bungalow was built here by Lewis Brundage as a showroom for Lake Keuka Floral Company. The large glass windows were filled with potted plants, palms, ferns and cut flowers. Brundage was an excellent florist and landscaper. His business thrived; he sold his plants wholesale and built two large greenhouses in the back. In

1938 they advertised cabbage, cauliflower, tomato, pepper, zinnia, aster, marigold and petunia plants for sale. The property included a great deal of land along Jacob's Brook. The building has been remodeled, but you can still see the lines of the original bungalow. It is now the Flour Shop, cafe and bakery.

Number 219. This Abraham Wagener lot was sold to Elizabeth Chapman in 1823. It was owned by many people over the years. In 1881 Delos Hollowell built his home here. He was half of the Hollowell & Wise Hardware Store which was on the south corner of Main and Elm Streets. They carried home furnishings, plumbing, steam and hot water heating systems, stoves and more. The house became a Methodist parsonage. Catholic Charities owns it now. The inside has beautiful oak and cherry woodwork including built in cupboards. There

219 Main Street (GRL)

are ornate brass door knobs, double doors with beveled glass and an ornate stained glass window on the north side. It is Queen Anne style.

217 Main Street (GRL)

Number 217 Main Street has been stripped of all its Queen Anne decoration. In 1814 Jonathan Bordwell owned the land from William Cornwell's (the south boundary of the Court Street extension) all the way to 163 Main. He was a partner with Miles Benham in a leather and shoe shop. Alexander M. Boyd bought the lot in 1837 and built this house. Boyd sold it to Charles C. Miller, who sold

173

it to Alexander F. Hazen in 1852. He made a lot of alterations. The original interior had two marble fireplaces, a black walnut staircase and banister, a black walnut bookcase with glass panel doors, gold stenciled porcelain door knobs and escutcheons. Hazen sold it to George McAllister, who in 1866 sold it to the Presbyterian Church for use as a parsonage.

215 Main Street, the Post House (GRL)

Number **215 Main** Street is now called the Post House. This Victorian was built in 1876 by Charles R. King who bought the property from Stewart Ellsworth. The Ellsworth house which had been on a large lot burned in 1871. They sold this part of the lot to King. King was an attorney and part of the firm Prosser and King. Ellsworth, one of the village's leading merchants, was involved in setting up stage routes and building the first steamboat on Keuka Lake. In 1884 the property was sold to Adelaide Post Briggs. In 1914 it was owned by Mary Leah Post. Its style is French Renaissance – inspired Gothic Revival. It is called the "Post House" for Mary Leah. Her first marriage was to Rexford Potter, son of Edson Potter. That marriage ended in divorce and she married into the wealthy Post family from the town of Seneca. The house is one of the most unusual in Penn Yan. Take time to study it. All the details have been kept. It has been converted from a family home to rental office space.

This house is a good example of stick style. Notice that the clapboarding is vertical in a board and batten style. The brackets are unique. The tower and the peaked gables are certainly interesting, and the tabbed decoration on the exterior is very special. The beautiful front door retains its original glass with bird motifs. The porch has chamfered posts and diagonal braces with spindle work on the balustrade above. There is a wealth of detail here. On the inside there were two marble fireplaces in the front parlor. The carriage house in the back has been converted into two apartments.

Number **213 Main**. A boarding house, three floors high with balconies or porches across the front of each floor once stood here. At that time there were four gorgeous houses in a row. The Presbyterian Church was on the corner. The church was rebuilt after it burned in 1958. When they built

213 Main Street (YCH)

the new church they took down the house at 213 Main to make room for parking. The old church, built in 1879, was square with a 100 foot steeple and could seat 1000. The house that at one time stood on that corner was 211 Main Street, built in 1841 by Nelson Tunnicliff and his wife Mary. He was a partner in the Stewart and Tunnicliff store, a

New Presbyterian Church building built after the 1958 fire (GRL)

175

54967 First Presbyterian Church, Penn Yan, N. Y.

211-213 Main Street, the 1st Presbyterian church building on this site. It was destroyed by fire in 1958. The first Presbyterian Church built in Penn Yan was located further up Main Street at 304 – 307. (YCGHS)

general merchandise store once located at 25 Main. They purchased all kinds of grain and produce, had a lot of warehouses, along with a line of canal boats. The house was sold to the **Presbyterian Church** in 1878 and torn down to build the first church on the site. A picture of that spectacular building is on the previous page.

179 Main Street - St. Mark's Episcopal Church. Around 1832 Samuel Curtiss built a five story commercial building at this location. He manufactured furniture and coffins there. He also

St. Mark's Episcopal Church today (SM)

rented out space to a weaver who made coverlets. On July 3, 1867 a fire, believed to have started in a nearby blacksmith shop, destroyed Curtiss' factory and the carriage works next door. St. Mark's parish had been incorporated in 1837. A church was built in 1838 on Main Street opposite the old Penn Yan Academy.

St. Mark's did not have regular rectors and the Civil War caused a split among the parishioners. Around 1870 a large group left and decided to organize another church to be called Grace Church. Those who remained were short of funds so the rectory and part of the church lot were sold and the lay reader left in charge. No regular services were held until 1875. A reorganization occurred during the next couple of years. Finances improved and the church was able to

St. Mark's Episcopal Church (foreground) and Penn Yan Presbyterian Church (background), 1909 (YCGHS)

179 Main Street, St. Mark's Episcopal Church with the original tower (YCGHS)

exchange their lot across from the Academy for that on the corner of Main and Clinton. A foundation was already here, laid by the parishioners who had left to found Grace Church. The new St. Mark's Episcopal Church opened its doors on October 30, 1879. The church further up Main Street was demolished. This situation is an interesting one — Grace Church provided the lot and St. Marks provided the funds to build the church. The church is English Gothic style. The original main entrance was the door on the north side of the tower. In 1888 they made plans to enlarge the church. It was at this time that the entrance was changed. In 1894 an organ was purchased and installed. Adding the organ meant that they had to enlarge the church. It was at this time they also straightened the south side. In 1940 a guildhall was built in the basement of the church. Ten years later the church broke ground for an addition for the parish hall which provided space for a kitchen, dining area and office space. In 1956 the tower was found to be unsafe and was replaced with what you see today.

175 Main Street. This land was owned by blacksmith George W. Johnson. It was in his shop that the fire started the night of July 3, 1867 which destroyed all the industrial buildings in the area. John H. Butler bought the lot from Ralph T. Wood in 1884 and built this substantial Queen Anne house. Butler was an attorney and the editor of the "Vineyardist." He sold the land to H. Allen Wagener in 1894. Allie Wagener was Abraham Wagener's great-grandson. It was his first home in Penn Yan. The house is Queen Anne in style. It has lost some of its original ornamentation. Still, notice the beautiful double door.

175 Main Street (SM)

Number **173 Main Street** — In 1800 this was the site of Abraham Wagener's first frame house. Later, in 1813 Abraham moved down the street to the Mansion House and his old house on this site was used as a hotel and a tavern

173 Main Street (GRL)

run by Mrs. Samuel Cobb. It burned in 1841. The site was then occupied by Wood & Bruen carriage makers. The carriage works were destroyed by the fire of 1867. After the fire, Dr. Robert Bordwell built this simple brick Italianate home. He sold the property to Andrew Whitaker in 1870. For many years the house was owned by Dr. G. Howard Leader the only eye, nose, ear and throat specialist in the county. He sold the house to dentists Hopestill R. Phillips and son-in-law Robert Wrean. Wrean was a former Confederate officer. Phillips' daughter, Virginia Phillips Wrean, was also a dentist and a part of the practice.

171 Main Street (SM)

Number **171 Main Street** was built by Dr. Nathan Lusk in 1876. The lot had contained part of the Wood & Bruen carriage works until the fire of 1867 destroyed it. In 1894 Dr. Lusk's wife Sarah sold the south half of the lot to Elsie Doubleday, wife of Dr. Charles E. Doubleday, for number 173. Be sure to notice the Eastlake carving above the windows. The double door with arabesque design was very typical of Penn Yan at that time. Notice the Italianate brackets and the General Grant turret with a metal top which still has its original slate roof. In addition to the Italianate features you also can see Second Empire and Gothic Revival influence. Dr. Nathan Lusk practiced medicine here in the late 19th Century. It was a single family residence until the 1990s.

Number **169 Main Street** has had a lot of changes over the years. It was built in 1854 by Henry Wood of Bruen and Wood. Nathaniel Ayre bought it from the Denton brothers in 1857. He

169 Main Street (GRL)

and his wife opened a private school here to teach deportment and general education to young ladies and gentlemen. Students could board at the school for $150.08 per year. After Penn Yan Academy was founded in 1859, the school's enrollment declined and Ayre moved to Philadelphia. Notice the beautiful porch on the side of the house with the lattice work and eyebrow windows, and the brackets along the roof. The eyebrow windows are unusual for Italianate architecture. It is said that this house originally had a metal roof and an octagonal cupola. It survived the fire of 1867. The house was later owned by Abraham Wagener's youngest daughter, Henrietta Monell and by members of the Sheppard family. Brothers George and Oliver Sheppard lived here and created wonderful scrap books of newspaper clippings about Penn Yan which are available at the Underwood House Museum on Chapel Street.

Number **167 Main Street**. The back portion of this house was originally Greek Revival in style and was built by John Bruen about 1848. He sold the property to Darius Adams who sold it to dry goods

167 Main Street (SM)

merchant George Cramer about 1867. Cramer added the front section with Italianate characteristics shortly after he bought the house. Notice the distinctive front door with the iron medallion panels. He also added the porches. Cramer opened the Empire Clothing Store in Penn Yan. In 1940 Mrs. Pearl Saxby of Corning bought the home and converted it into a tea room and tourist home.

Number **165 Main** was built before 1825 by Miles Benham. It is a good example of an early Federal style commercial building. You can see that the roof has very little overhang which is typical of Federal style. The Victorian porches were added later. Notice the step gables. In the 1820s it was owned by the Benham family business. They owned all the way down to Jacob's Brook. It may have been used as a tavern in 1823. In 1850 Miles Benham operated a leather and shoe shop here. About 1860 it was owned by James

165 Main Street (GRL)

D. Morgan who owned the first hardware store in Penn Yan where 101 Main Street is today.

In 1882 it was A. B. Pierce's Hotel. Next it became a boarding house. In 1884 Dr. W. C. Allen had his medical practice here. In 1888 it belonged to Dr. Franklin S. Sampson. He was the man who built Sampson's Theater on East Elm Street. In 1909 Doctors Frank and Alan Sampson bought the house. Then in 1929 it was purchased by Dr. E. Carlton Foster and Dr. John A. Hatch. It housed the offices of Foster-Hatch Medical Group from 1929 to 1977. They had one of the first group medical practices in the United States. Medical and surgical services were available early morning till late at night. They had x-ray equipment and a laboratory. Their staff had only the best training.

163 Main Street was built in 1954 for W. T. Grant Company, department store. They closed in 1975. In 1980 the building was taken over by Birkett Mills. It was renovated and used by Birkett Mills for their offices and testing kitchen. The building replaced a Victorian Gothic house built in the 1880s. The last owners of the house were Fred and Lulu Guyle. Fred was a local state trooper and

163 Main Street today (GRL)

163 Main Street before being replaced with the W.T. Grant Company building (YCH)

had his office in his home. Lulu was Yates county's first female county clerk. That house was razed in 1953.

We are now back where we started. This concludes our tour of Penn Yan's Main Street. We hope that you have enjoyed learning about the village, its buildings and its people. Penn Yan's historic district has many stories to tell. Its buildings are like people, each unique.

As you learn about the past you cannot help but appreciate the present. When you think back to what it was like for the first settlers who traveled to the Genesee Country you realize what hard work it was to create this village, its buildings, its institutions and all that we take for granted. Life in the early days was not easy. The first settlers did not have access to modern tools, equipment, transportation, or even easy methods of communication with the outside world. They could not go down to the corner store and purchase food, clothing, or furniture. There was no electricity, no refrigeration, no washing machines. Heat came from a wood fire. Much has changed over the years and we have a great deal to be thankful for. We have barely scratched the surface of what life was like in the early days of Penn

Yan. There are many interesting stories about the village and how life changed over the years for its residents. If you want to learn more about Penn Yan and the region's history be sure to take advantage of this area's many historical societies and museums. Make time to discover the past, and its influence on the present. You will be glad you did.

Sources

Historic Main Street, A Walking Tour – Yates County Chamber of Commerce with help from Frances Dumas, Yates County Historian

Aspiring Christians, Histories of Yates County Churches – Compiled by Linda J. Jackson 1998

A Good Country, A Pleasant Habitation, ©1990 text and graphics Frances Dumas, maps ©1990 Frances Dumas and Patricia Rios

The Sesquicentennial History of Penn Yan, New York 1833 – 1983, ©1983 Yates County Genealogical & Historical Society, compiled from the archives of the Yates County Genealogical & Historical Society and from the private collection of Mrs. Catharine Spencer

It Started With A Steamboat, An American Saga by Steven Harvey ©2007, ISBN: 1-4208-4943-3 Authorhouse

History of Penn Yan by Walter Wolcott c.1914

The Outlet Trail by Frances Dumas ©1984 and 1992

And In Penn Yan, When You Get To the Corner by Dennis K. Murphy and D. A. Mills ©1976 JKM Printing, Branchport, NY 14418

But I Always Called Her Mama by Dennis K. Murphy and Donald A. Mills 1979 JKM Printing Co., Branchport, NY 14418

The Natural Science Camp at Tichenor Point Canandaigua Lake, Canandaigua 1890 – 1905 by Ray Henry, Town of Canandaigua Historian, 2010, published by Ontario County Historical Society

Images of America KEUKA LAKE by Charles R. Mitchell, 2002 Arcadia Publishing

Building Structure Inventory Forms, Division for Historic Preservation, NYS Parks and Recreation January 1979
Site #123-40-0063, Roger G. Reed, Yates County Historical Society

Penn Yan New York Directory ©1927, compiled and published by H.A. Manning Company

Stark's Penn Yan Directory 1935, Penn Yan Printing Company

Penn Yan, NY & Rural Routes Directory 1938 compiled and published by the Hogan Directory Company, Binghamton, NY

Penn Yan Sanborn Map & Publishing Company – 1886, 1892, 1897, 1903, 1909, 1922, 1931, 1931-1950 maps

Parsons Penn Yan, Dundee and Yates County Directory 1889 – published by The Journal Company, Printers & Binders

Parsons Penn Yan, Dundee & Yates County Directory 1892 – 1893 Samuel Parsons Directory Publisher, Syracuse 1892

Chatford's County Directory 1894 (This directory is a part of the YCGHS archives and does not have the front page listing the publisher and their location.)

Penn Yan N.Y. Directory 1913 compiled and published by Calkin-Kelly Directory Company, Binghamton, NY

History of Yates County, NY Edited by Lewis Cass Aldrich, Syracuse NY, D. Mason & Co. Publishers 1892

Little Yates And The United States by Ralph W. Seager, 1976, Tillman Press Inc., Penn Yan, NY

Directory of the Owners of Cottages and Lake Front Homes on Keuka Lake published by John V. Stark, Penn Yan 1935

The Yates Lumber Co. basket catalog printed by O. J. Townsend, Penn Yan, New York date unknown

Combination Atlas Map of Yates County New York, compiled, drawn and published from personal examinations and surveys, Everts, Ensign & Everts, Philadelphia 1876

The Lost Resort Lucile Peterson Macera, Shirley Know VanDyne, & Merlyn H. Wheeler Jr., Heart of the Lakes Publishing, Interlaken, NY 1993

George Sheppard's scrap books of newspaper clippings for the years: 1904, 1905, 1906, 1907, 1909, 1916, 1917, 1918, 1920, 1921, 1922, 1927, 1928, 1929, 1930, 1931, 1932, 1933, 1934, 1935, 1937, 1938 available at the Underwood House, a part of the Yates County Genealogical & Historical Society, Penn Yan, New York 14527

Chronicle & New Age 1917

Yates County Chronicle 1920

Chronicle Express 1930, 1936

Penn Yan Democrat 1931, 1938

www.pyhistory.org

www.history.rochester.edu/canal

www.yatescounty.org

www.freethought-trail.org

www.ioof.org

www.measuringworth.com

www.oneidaindiannation.com

http://thebirkettmills.com

http://en.wikipedia.org/wiki/Wilmot_Proviso

http://steamtraction.farmcollector.com/company-history

http://www.sampsontheatre.org

http://freepages.history.rootswen.ancestry.com

http://www.keukayc.org/KYC-history.html

http://www.winepros.org/wine101/history.htm

The Archives of the Yates County Genealogical & Historical Society, Penn Yan, New York 14527

We greatly appreciate the ability to reprint the images that appear in this book. Each image's source is indicated with initials as depicted below or the source is a part of the copy below the image. Images came from the following sources:

1. Courtesy of the Yates County Genealogical & Historical Society (YCGHS)

2. Courtesy of the Dundee Area Historical Society (DAHS)

3. 2010-2012 Photographs taken by Gerald R. Lange (GRL)

4. 2010-2012 Photographs taken by Sid Mann (SM)

5. *The Combination Atlas Map of Yates County New York 1876*

6. Walter Wolcott's book *History of Penn Yan*, 1917 (Wolcott)

7. Yates County Historian's office (YCH)

8. Penn Yan Sanborn maps from the years 1886, 1903 and 1931

9. Building Structure Inventory Forms of the Historic Preservation District (HP)

10. Tom Packard Collection (TPC)

11. Ted Henry, cinematographer of 1940 Penn Yan movie/Penn Yan Kiwanis Club (TH/PYK)

12. Penn Yan's History website www.pyhistory.org developed by Frances Dumas, the Penn Yan Village Historian (PYHist) c. 2007

13. Bob Scharf Collection (BSC)

A WALK ALONG PENN YAN'S MAIN STREET
CHILDREN'S SCAVENGER HUNT

When you have answered all the questions, *carefully* remove this quiz and hand it in at the back counter of Long's Card & Books to receive your prize.

SITE	QUESTION
Hendersons Drugs 126 Main St.	What was the name of the business that was once located here? Look on the wall for the picture. _____
Pinckney Hardware 24 Main St.	What hardware store was located here when Pinckney's purchased the building? Look for a picture at the cash register. _____
Birkett Mills Corner of Seneca & Main Streets	When was the large pancake made? _____
Angel's Restaurant 5 Main St. *Open 'till 3:00pm*	Angel's was once the Stratton's Restaurant. What did 3 donuts cost in 1930? Check the menu on the wall behind the counter. _____

191

SITE	QUESTION
Milly's Pantry 19 Main St.	What do the IOOF's three rings stand for? Check the walls for the answer.
	_____
The Nest Egg Gift Shop 125 Main St.	A drug store was once located here. What was it's name? Check for a frame with the answer.
	_____
Yates County Arts Center 127 Main St.	This building was built as a bank in 1872. What was the name of that bank? Look for a framed image of that bank.
	_____
Long's Cards & Books 115 Main St.	On the second floor is the old Cornwell Opera House and Lecture Hall. Who once spoke here? Look for a frame that shows the answer.
	_____